SCOTLAND'S COUNTRYSIDE

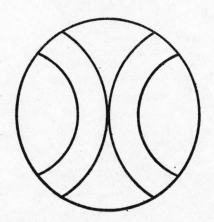

**THE OFFICIAL GUIDE PUBLISHED BY THE
COUNTRYSIDE COMMISSION FOR SCOTLAND,
BATTLEBY, REDGORTON, PERTH**

A

ACKNOWLEDGEMENTS

Many individuals and organisations have assisted the Countryside Commission for Scotland in the preparation of this book, and the Commission are grateful for their co-operation.

Thanks are due to Shell-Mex and BP Ltd. for the generous offer of assistance which made the atlas section possible and for permission to use their copyright maps, and to Mr John Flower for permission to use his cartography.

The National Trust for Scotland and the Department of the Environment have given help at many stages in the preparation of the book; the Commission are grateful to the Trust for allowing the use of their material and to the Controller of HMSO for permission to base descriptive notes on material included in "The Illustrated Guide to Ancient Monuments in Scotland" Vol 6.

The Commission also wish to thank Don Aldridge for the line drawings; and the following organisations for the use of photographs: the National Trust for Scotland; the Nature Conservancy Council; the Forestry Commission; and individual photographers as credited. The cover picture of Loch Tulla is reproduced by courtesy of the Scottish Field.

© 1974 Countryside Commission for Scotland
Maps © Shell-Mex BP Ltd. Photo copyrights as credited
ISBN 902226 22 3

CONTENTS

PLEASE Follow the Country Code
When you are in the countryside always remember to:

GUARD AGAINST ALL RISK OF FIRE

FASTEN ALL GATES

KEEP DOGS UNDER PROPER CONTROL

KEEP TO THE PATHS ACROSS FARM LAND

AVOID DAMAGING FENCES, HEDGES AND WALLS

LEAVE NO LITTER

SAFEGUARD WATER SUPPLIES

PROTECT WILDLIFE, WILD PLANTS AND TREES

GO CAREFULLY ON COUNTRY ROADS

RESPECT THE LIFE OF THE COUNTRYSIDE

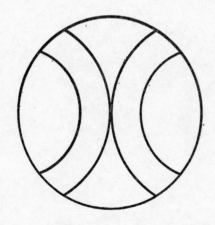

CONSERVING SCOTLAND'S COUNTRYSIDE

CONSERVING SCOTLAND'S COUNTRYSIDE

WHY DO WE VISIT SCOTLAND'S COUNTRYSIDE?

In 1972 6¼ million UK residents and over 800,000 overseas visitors spent holidays in Scotland. What did they come to find and what do we, the 5¼ million people living in Scotland, seek on our increasingly frequent trips into the Scottish countryside?

Probably most people would put scenery at the top of the list. But others will be looking for freedom to enjoy outdoor activities, or the chance to watch wild birds and animals in their natural surroundings or to visit places of interest that will help to bring alive the story of Scotland's past. And at least a few will undoubtedly be seeking peace and quiet or solitude, with an opportunity to "get right away from it all".

WILL IT ALWAYS BE THERE TO VISIT?

At present the Scottish countryside fulfils a variety of functions. It is a "factory" for the important and basic production industries of farming and forestry. It provides a home for a large population of birds and animals and for the plants and insects that they depend upon. And it serves as a recreational resource for growing numbers of people.

But will the countryside always be able to satisfy all these – and many other – different needs? What about the effects of "progress" in the shape of new motorways, provisions for tourists, industrial demands such as the currently topical oil-related developments and so on? How much longer can all the needs continue to be accommodated side by side in the Scottish countryside or are there some things that just cannot go together?

WHERE DO THE CONFLICTS LIE?

Some of the incompatibles are immediately identifiable. Motorways and housing developments take land from the farmer and this kind of change in land-use is seldom reversible. So food production may suffer as a result of development. And it is worth noting in this connection that Scotland has only a limited amount of first class arable land and much of this lies along the east coast where development is proceeding apace.

The potential conflict between different needs is not always so clear-cut however and sometimes the extent to which different demands on the countryside are in conflict is largely a matter of degree. Let us take a freshwater loch as an example. A few fishermen, either in boats or on the shore, or the odd sailing dinghy, will probably have little effect on the water birds feeding and nesting in the area. But introduce regular flotillas of fishermen and sailing dinghies and there will be an immediate decrease in the local wildlife.

Some people might ask "what does that matter?" The answer we give to questions regarding land-use and the priority that should be given to different demands is likely to be prefaced by the phrase "it all depends". It all depends on what sort of future we see for mankind. On whether we regard economic progress as the most important consideration or whether we believe that it also matters that people should be able to enjoy countryside recreation of many different types. Whether we think that any one recreational interest has a greater right to be satisfied than the others and whether we agree with the view that the conservation of amenity and wildlife is a matter that concerns us all.

3

One point on which we are all likely to be in agreement is the need for Scotland to provide homes and jobs, transport and other facilities for her own people, as well as providing recreation space for them and for many others as well. Inevitably, many developments will take place in what is at present "countryside", effectively decreasing the amount of land available for other purposes. If the Scotland's countryside of the future is to be capable of continuing to satisfy our varied needs, it is essential that everything possible is done to minimise conflicts between different interests and demands.

WHAT CAN PLANNING DO TO HELP?

If we accept that each and every demand upon Scotland's countryside should be met *somewhere* within the country we at once find ourselves faced with the question "where?". Answering this question presents the land-use planners with many problems of conflicting interests and quite a number of these become news items when they give rise to public local inquiries. Very often such public inquiries result from proposals for industrial development in a predominantly rural setting, a situation which frequently arouses strong local feelings. The prospects of short-term gain and the likely long-term effect on an area are seldom easy to assess reliably — and there can be few among us who could claim to make an utterly unbiased judgment when our own immediate interests are at stake!

It is natural human behaviour to kick against restrictions, and the introduction be planning controls necessarily implies some restrictions on the use to which land may to put. Nevertheless controls designed to ensure that land is used in the most appropriate way can be of great help in determining whether any particular demand should be met in a specific place, and in preventing wasteful use of limited resources.

Basically, countryside planning in its widest sense is concerned first and foremost with the identification of areas in which particular developments should or should not be allowed. For example, each local planning authority, in its Development Plan, identifies those areas in which it will actively encourage industrial development and those in which such development will be discouraged. When the general pattern for permitted use has been established the planners can get down to considering such questions as "is the architectural character of this part of village X worth preserving?", or "should this estuary become a local nature reserve?", or "how can we best develop this area for public recreational use?".

In the past 25 years various ways of planning countryside land-use and various designations relating to its use for specific purposes have been introduced in Scotland. Some apply south of the Border as well as in Scotland and some do not; some result from legislation and some do not. The one thing they have in common is that they all have a part to play in reconciling conflicting demands.

LOOKING AFTER THE LANDSCAPE

One of Scotland's best known assets is her scenery, which is notable not only for the grandeur of its mountains and the wildness of its coastal cliffs but also for the remarkable variety of landscape to be found within quite a small area. What can be done to ensure that the most attractive areas of Scotland are protected from unsuitable development? We come up against another problem here — who is to decide which are "the most attractive areas" and how is the decision to be reached?

The evaluation of landscape is to a considerable extent a matter of personal preference but it will also be influenced by the relative scarcity or abundance of similar scenery in the vicinity. It is, for example, no easy matter to identify the most attractive stretches of countryside in a county which has a vast expanse of mountain, glen and sea-loch.

4

The demands made on the Scottish countryside today are many and varied. Some of them, such as motorway and housing developments, take land away from the basic industries of farming and forestry and involve changes in land-use that are seldom reversible. (Photo: Kelty by-pass — Scottish Field)

For many people the main attraction of the Scottish countryside is its scenery
For a few it is the opportunity to find solitude "away from it all".
(Photo: The Cairngorms seen from Carn an Righ – John Watt)

Others are looking for freedom to enjoy more gregarious outdoor activities.
This ever-growing demand for recreation space puts considerable pressure on
the countryside's wildlife. (Photo: Young canoeists on Loch Lomond –
V. M. Thom)

Some kinds of plant-life, especially wet-land vegetation, are easily destroyed by trampling. Nature reserves of this kind are consequently unsuitable for extensive public use. (Photo: Bog plants on Inverpolly NNR — Nature Conservancy Council)

Many birds and animals are similarly vulnerable to disturbance. Their future will depend upon the existence of reserves or sanctuaries where they are safe from constant human interruption. (Photo: Greylag geese on a Border loch — C. K. Mylne)

*Wildlife conservation will depend increasingly upon whether wildlife enthusiasts exercise restraint in the pursuit of their interests. Rare birds are best looked for **outside** the breeding season; photographs of flowers are preferable to dried specimens. (Photo: Nature photography student in action – Brian Bracegirdle)*

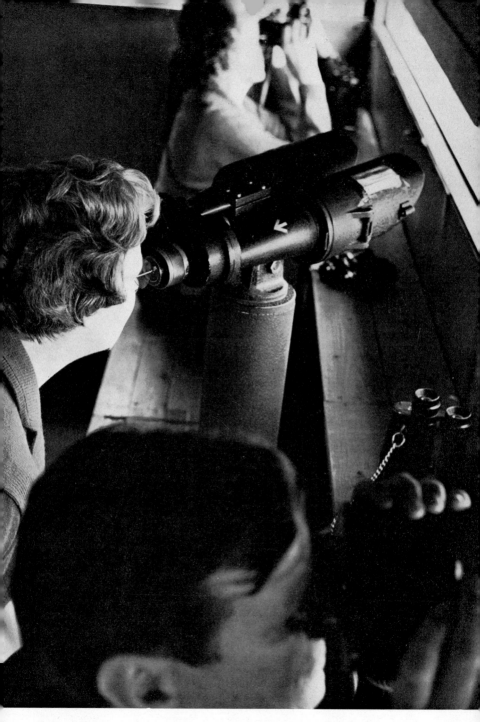

On some nature reserves it has been possible to make special arrangements so that large numbers of people can see and enjoy the wildlife of the reserve without disturbing it. (Photo: Watching wildlife from a SWT hide – Scottish Field)

By following nature trails, visitors to the countryside can increase their understanding of what is special about an area's wildlife.
(Photo: Landmark Nature Trail — David Hayes)

Facilities for more detailed study of wildlife exist on some nature reserves and school parties are increasingly making use of such opportunities.
(Photo: A Glasgow school party at Ardmore Reserve — C. K. Mylne)

For those seeking walking routes in the Scottish countryside there are, in addition to the old-established right of way paths, a growing number of sign-posted walkways and forest walks. (Photo: An early Scottish Rights of Way Society signpost – Scottish Field)

Inexperienced parties should not make expeditions into mountainous country unless they are accompanied by a countryside ranger or suitably qualified leader. (Photo: A climbing party in the Torridon hills – National Trust for Scotland)

Scotland's Forest Parks, which include both afforested ground and open country, provide many and varied opportunities for outdoor recreation. The restriction of vehicles to selected areas helps to preserve the peace and unspoilt character of these parks. (Photo: Argyll Forest Park – Forestry Commission)

Forests, more than any other form of land-use, can absorb large numbers of people into the countryside without injuring the environment. Recognising this fact the Forestry Commission provides recreational facilities in many of its forest properties. (Photo: Cashel Caravan Site, Loch Lomond – Forestry Commission)

When the local planning authorities were invited by the Secretary of State for Scotland to identify, in their County Development Plans, those stretches of countryside which they proposed to designate as Areas of Great Landscape Value (AGLVs), they experienced just this sort of difficulty, with the result that the identified AGLVs are very unevenly distributed and are surprisingly sparse in parts of Scotland which most people would consider to be of high landscape value.

To assist with future attempts at landscape evaluation the Countryside Commission for Scotland has been working on the development of a more objective appraisal system, in which subjective personal assessments are replaced by a methodical consideration of the various elements that make up the landscape.

An important method of safeguarding the countryside against the spread of urban sprawl is by the designation of Green Belts. These are stretches of land which lie close to built-up areas but which are themselves "countryside" in character. Restriction of developments within the Green Belts to those associated with agriculture, horticulture, private open space or recreation can effectively ensure that neighbouring towns do not continue expanding until they merge.

Many of Scotland's villages, with their buildings of distinctive character and architectural interest, add greatly to the appearance of the landscape. The character of such villages can be all too easily destroyed by unsympathetic modern buildings. To protect them from undesirable developments a number of Scottish villages have been declared "Conservation Areas" in which all new buildings or modernisations of old ones must be particularly carefully designed to blend into the existing character of the area.

It is not, of course, enough just to look after the Areas of Great Landscape Value, the Green Belts and the Conservation Areas and to allow any type of development to take place in the countryside in-between without restriction or control. The normal planning procedures in practice ensure that this should not happen and increasing attention is now paid to the need for careful siting of large buildings and for the landscaping and screening of structures which are likely to stand out as obtrusive elements in the landscape.

Planning permission for new developments nowadays frequently includes a requirement relating to tree planting in the vicinity. The value of trees and shrubs, not only as screening for buildings but also as an amenity in their own right and as habitats for wildlife, is now widely recognised, and the introduction of "instant tree" techniques, whereby well-grown trees can be transplanted, has greatly speeded up the establishment of effective woodland screens and amenity areas. This does not mean, however, that we should consider existing trees and woodlands as expendable. The application of Tree Preservation Orders is one way of ensuring that small patches of woodland, attractive rows of trees or even particularly fine individual specimens are not felled for reasons of convenience during the construction of housing schemes or other developments.

In addition to the planning controls already mentioned a watching brief over the 98% of Scotland officially designated as countryside is kept by the Countryside Commission for Scotland. This body has a special duty to keep under review all matters relating to the provision of facilities for the enjoyment of the countryside and the conservation and enhancement of its natural beauty and amenity.

These, then, are the principal ways in which Scotland's landscape is safeguarded today but is there, perhaps, something missing?

WHY HAS SCOTLAND NO NATIONAL PARKS?

To many people the most appropriate way to look after the landscape on the grand scale appears to be through the creation of National Parks. The knowledge that Scotland, with so much magnificent scenery to cherish, has at present no National Parks consequently comes as a great surprise to some people.

Opinions on exactly what a National Park should be and what purpose it should fulfil have changed considerably since the idea was first conceived over a hundred years ago in the United States. In those days pressures on the countryside were very much less than they are today and it was quite realistic to suggest that to maintain a large stretch of country in a "wild" and "natural" condition and to ensure its perpetual availability for public use and recreation were compatible objectives.

But what has happened in the USA during the last one hundred years? The size of the population and its mobility have increased enormously. There has been a corresponding increase in the demand for facilities such as roads, accommodation and camp sites within the National Parks. And the very pressure of public interest in. and use of, the Parks is now making it progressively more difficult to protect their "wild" and "natural" character and even to prevent irreparable damage being done to some of their most important natural and historic sites.

It appears, then, that it is no longer realistic to expect to achieve nature conservation and unrestricted public use in one and the same area. To which objective should priority be given or is there any way in which a compromise could be reached? During the National Parks Centenary Year in 1972 it was agreed internationally that a system of zoning within Parks was required.

The aim of zoning would be to ensure that the usage of any area was related to the capacity of that area to withstand visitor pressure. Before zoning could be introduced it would be necessary to survey the whole Park, assessing the comparative ability of different landscapes and vegetation types to screen developments and to survive foot and vehicular traffic. Implementation of the zoning system would then involve the designation of special tourism zones in which the facilities necessary for the reception of the visiting public could be located. A "buffer" zone might surround the tourism area, protecting the remoter parts of the Park from disturbance and ensuring that the primary function of nature conservation could be carried on there with a minimum of interference. Only in the tourism zone would access by vehicle be allowed.

There have been National Parks in England and Wales for nearly 25 years now and they too have experienced the problems brought by increasing numbers of visitors. But because these Parks include substantial areas of farmland and other "managed" countryside, along with a considerable resident population, nature conservation has been considered as a secondary function and the provision of recreation space has been seen as of greater importance.

We now come back to our earlier question, why has Scotland no National Parks? Briefly, the explanation is one of historical fact. When the National Parks and Access to the Countryside Act was introduced in 1949 the section authorising the designation of National Parks applied only to England and Wales, and not to Scotland. This was partly due to the fact that in Scotland access to open country had always been easier and population pressures less than in England and Wales, where there was an increasing demand for action towards solving access problems. This demand came from both landowners and recreational interests, the former emphasising the need for control over access and the latter demanding greater freedom of access.

Whatever the reason for the anomaly, the legal situation is still the same today, with no legislation enabling the designation of National Parks in Scotland. Five areas considered to have potential as National Parks were, however, identified as long ago as 1948 and officially designated as National Park Direction Areas. This designation affords some protection to the natural beauty and amenity of these areas, through special planning oversight, but it does not give the public any special rights of access within the area.

Although there are at present no Scottish National Parks, there have for some time been Forest Parks, the first of which dates from 1935, some 15 years before the first National Park was developed in England. Between them the five Scottish Forest Parks cover 300,000 acres of fine scenery and fulfil many of the functions of National Parks.

The Forestry Commission created its Forest Parks in the belief that where land was acquired in connection with the planting of new forests it should remain open for public enjoyment. Much of this land is, of course, tree covered but there are also large areas within the Parks which, for a variety of reasons, will never be planted and will continue under farming, sporting or recreational use. By the restriction of private vehicles to those forest roads that provide access to recreational facilities, tourist pressures are effectively localised and the main area of the Parks remains peaceful and unspoilt for those travelling on foot.

The question of whether or not it is either necessary or desirable to create National Parks in Scotland remains then a topic for discussion and debate. Would designation attract so much additional attention to a park area that the resultant pressure would make protection of the park's landscape and wildlife an impossible task, and would destroy the quality of experience that the visitor comes for? Could a practicable zoning system be devised and implemented so as to ensure that the "people pressure" is localised and that substantial parts of the park remain undisturbed? Until satisfactory answers can be provided to these and many other questions we should perhaps be thankful that separate arrangements designed either to conserve wildlife or to provide for people in the countryside already exist.

CONSERVING WILDLIFE

Within Scotland's countryside there is a tremendous variety of wildlife. All of it, from ancient pine tree to tiny lichen and from majestic golden eagle to St Kilda's special mouse, contributes not only to the way the countryside looks but also to its biological balance. And all of it must find living space in the Scottish countryside. What is being done, then, to ensure that the needs of wildlife are adequately catered for amidst the increasing pressures of today?

First, we have the National Nature Reserves, which are looked after by the Nature Conservancy Council. These are stretches of land, ranging from 12 to over 64,000 acres in extent, scattered widely over the country. They represent samples of the most important types of wildlife habitats in Scotland or examples of particularly important geological formations. They have been created in order to maintain these sample areas free from outside interference and to provide opportunities within them for the scientific study of the inter-relationships between plants and animals and their physical surroundings.

The National Nature Reserves (NNRs) are essentially places for wildlife. Many of them are very vulnerable to damage by trampling and disturbance, and are consequently unsuitable for extensive public use. On some reserves, however, arrangements have been made for receiving visitors and helping them to understand what is special about the reserve's wildlife and these reserves are indicated on Map 1.

We also have several other kinds of nature reserves in Scotland. There are two Local Nature Reserves, established by local authorities, at Aberlady Bay, East Lothian and at Castle and Hightae Lochs, Dumfriesshire, and there is a Forest Nature Reserve at Glen Nant in Argyll. There is also a growing number of reserves created by voluntary organisations such as the Scottish Wildlife Trust and the Royal Society for the Protection of Birds. Like the NNRs, these reserves have been created primarily to ensure protection for a wide variety of habitats and for the individual species of plants, birds and animals associated with them, but a few have been developed in such a way that large numbers of people can visit them without causing disturbance to the wildlife. (Map 1)

As well as being responsible for National Nature Reserves the Nature Conservancy Council have a duty to inform local planning authorities of areas considered to be of special scientific interest but which are not included in a nature reserve. Designation as a Site of Special Scientific Interest gives some degree of protection since all development proposals for these areas must be referred to the Nature Conservancy Council for its views. The term "development" in this context does not, however, include agricultural or forestry operations and there is consequently no safeguard against damage to the scientific interest of a site through operations such as drainage or tree planting.

There are, of course, some forms of wildlife which require special protection at certain times of the year or in certain places. In the case of birds there are various ways of ensuring that this is given. One way is to establish a statutory Bird Sanctuary, in which all species of bird are fully protected throughout the year. (The Protection of Birds Acts provide protection to virtually all birds during the breeding season but allow certain kinds to be shot at other times). Sanctuaries, where public access is restricted, are particularly helpful in such places as small islands with large populations of ground-nesting birds, or in wetland areas where disturbance of the vegetation may cause losses of eggs and chicks. For ducks and geese, a place where they can roost undisturbed is particularly important, especially in areas where there is extensive wildfowling. Several Scottish lochs are among the areas which have been designated as wildfowl refuges to provide this rather specialised form of protection.

WILDLIFE CONSERVATION OUTSIDE THE DESIGNATED AREAS

There are, then, quite a number of different ways of conserving wildlife in particular places. But what about all the in-between bits of the Scottish countryside? What protection is given to wildlife outside the specially designated areas?

There is not space here to give a full answer to the legal side of this question, as there are many different laws related either directly or indirectly to the protection of wildlife. It is sufficient simply to say that there are already laws to protect birds and to ensure regular close seasons for game animals; to prevent the burning of moorland during the nesting season and to control the use of snares, traps and poison; and that laws to protect badgers and wild plants are in process of introduction.

MAP 1: SOME NATURE RESERVES WITH EDUCATIONAL PROVISIONS

Key   ◯ Information/Interpretation Centre   ❊ Nature Trail

      ● Field Study Centre   ▦ Hide

1. Caerlaverock/East Park	10. Loch an Eilein
2. Loch Leven Nature Centre	11. Craigellachie
3. Isle of May	12. Loch Garten
4. Ardmore Point	13. Beinn Eighe
5. Inchcailloch	14. Inverpolly
6. Loch of the Lowes	15. Handa
7. St. Cyrus	16. Copinsay
8. Strontian Glen/Ariundle	17. Fetlar
9. Rhum	

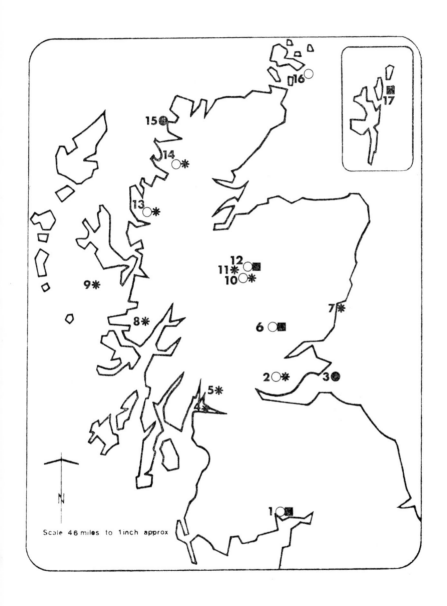

But legal protection and designated wildlife areas are only part of the picture; even more important is the contribution made by those who manage the land. Reserves can only go so far towards maintaining Scotland's wildlife; its future will depend increasingly on what happens in the in-between areas. Whether farmers and land-owners continue to consider conservation of wildlife and amenity to be important; whether we who use the countryside for recreation are alive to the damage and destruction we can cause through thoughtlessness; and whether wildlife enthusiasts exercise restraint in the pursuit of their interests and resist the temptation to collect plants or visit the nesting sites of birds.

Collecting and "rarity-hunting" create considerable problems where wildlife conservation is concerned. It is natural enough for people to want to see eagles, ospreys, wildcats and so on, or to take home specimens of attractive wildflowers. But these activities present a very real threat to the objects of attention. Plant collecting can quite quickly destroy the local population of a species that reproduces only slowly. Visiting the nesting sites of birds can cause desertion and the loss of eggs through chilling or exposure to predators. We encourage people to become more interested in natural history, yet as they do so this problem becomes progressively greater.

The only real solution here must surely be the exercise of self-discipline. Colour photographs of flowers have many advantages over dried specimens. Rare birds need not be looked for during the breeding season. The more spectacular birds and animals are seldom easy to see under entirely natural conditions but close-up views of them can be readily obtained in wildlife parks. The creation of wildlife parks containing examples of Scotland's native fauna is one way of helping to satisfy the growing desire to see these creatures "in the flesh". In a sense these parks are a link between conserving wildlife and planning for people in the countryside.

PLANNING FOR PEOPLE

With so many more of us now owning cars and having longer holidays there has been a rapid increase in the demand for places in the countryside where we can picnic, allow the children to play in woodland or by water, or go for good long walks. The basic need here is for places where we know that our presence is not going to cause problems for other land-users. Exactly what is being done to satisfy this ever-growing demand?

Probably the most significant recent development resulted from the Countryside (Scotland) Act 1967. In addition to establishing the Countryside Commission for Scotland this Act authorised the creation of Country Parks. A Country Park, to quote the Act, is "a park or pleasure ground in the countryside which...... affords convenient opportunity to the public for enjoyment of the countryside or open air recreation." In other words it is a place in which the recreational needs of people receive priority, although consideration will also be given to the conservation of wildlife and amenity.

The Country Parks already established in Scotland, or in course of preparation, (see Map 2) vary widely in size and character. The attractions they offer include the policy grounds of Culzean Castle, water-based recreation in Renfrewshire, a wooded dell in Midlothian and a display of native animals in Dunbartonshire. All of these parks have a ranger-service able to supply us, the visiting public, with information and advice on where to go and what to do. Most have picnic areas and many have nature trails and visitor centres designed to stimulate our interest in the area, to help answer our questions and to increase our enjoyment.

Amongst the organisations providing "places for people" in the countryside, the National Trust for Scotland plays a major part. In addition to caring for a wide variety of historic buildings, the Trust also looks after extensive countryside properties (Map 2). These include islands, waterfalls, lochs and areas of mountainous country. Public access to the mountainous areas is unrestricted and at most of them facilities such as visitor centres and ranger services are provided for the benefit of the visitors.

The Forestry Commission, which is Scotland's largest landowner, plays an increasingly important role as a provider of recreation space. Forests, more than any other form of land-use, can absorb large numbers of people into the countryside without injuring the environment or interfering with the production of timber. Recognising this fact the Commission, in addition to creating the Forest Parks referred to earlier, welcomes the public, on foot, into most of its forests.

The forests themselves offer opportunities for various pursuits, such as loch and river fishing, sailing and canoeing, deer-stalking, pony-trekking and orienteering. A number of Forest Gardens and Arboreta are open to the public and the recreational facilities provided include camp sites and picnic sites, forest walks, viewpoints and information centres.

Away from the areas actively developed for recreation there is always a need to guard against the risk of fire or of delay to routine forest work. For this reason camping, vehicles and pony-trekking are allowed only in areas or on routes specially set aside for the purpose.

There are then, quite large stretches of countryside now available to us at all times for recreation. But what about all the rest of the Scottish countryside? What facilities are there for us to use in the areas where there are no Country Parks, Forest Parks or National Trust for Scotland countryside properties?

There are, of course, many old-established right of way paths, the most important of which are being signposted by the Scottish Rights of Way Society. Some work has been done recently to supplement these routes, most of which are relatively far from the built-up areas, by creating new walkways in the neighbourhood of towns and cities. Several disused railway lines have been adapted for this purpose, canal tow paths have been cleared and surfaced and in Glasgow a start has been made on a comprehensive system of walkways linking the city's parks and leading outwards to the surrounding countryside.

Another exciting development in this line is the "West Highland Way" proposed by the Countryside Commission for Scotland. This is a long-distance route which will run from Milngavie, on the outskirts of Glasgow, along the east shore of Loch Lomond and on through the hills to Fort William.

Most of us, however, are likely to be quite content with the short walks and viewpoints associated with many of the picnic sites now appearing in attractive countryside settings. There are, too, the many places of historic interest to visit, ranging from inhabited and fully furnished castles to standing stones over three thousand years old and to croft cottages looking just as they did a hundred years ago. And they are just as important a part of Scotland's countryside as are her mountain grandeur and her soaring eagles—and equally worth cherishing.

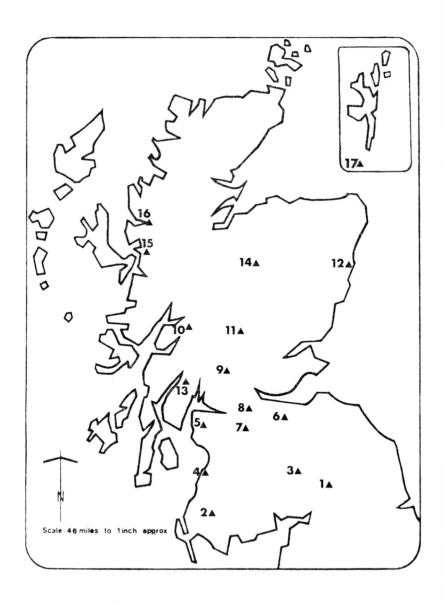

Scale : 46 miles to 1 inch approx

MAP 2   SOME PLACES FOR PEOPLE ▲

1. Border Forest Park
2. Galloway Forest Park
3. Grey Mare's Tail (NTS)
4. Culzean Country Park
5. Renfrew Regional Park
6. Almondell & Calder Country Park
7. Strathclyde Park (in preparation)
8. Palacerigg Country Park
9. Queen Elizabeth Forest Park
10. Glencoe (NTS)
11. Ben Lawers (NTS)
12. Loirston Park (in preparation)
13. Argyll Forest Park
14. Glenmore Forest Park
15. Balmacara and Kintail (NTS)
16. Torridon (NTS)
17. Fair Isle (NTS)

WHAT CAN WE DO TO HELP?

In each succeeding year more money and more effort are put into the conservation of our Scottish heritage and into making more of it accessible to all of us. Increasingly there is scope for every one of us to help with this task. We can help by remembering that the countryside is not just a place for recreation or wildlife but is also a "factory" from which farmers, foresters and landowners obtain a living, and which produces such basic essentials as food and timber. We can help by following the Country Code (see p iv) and by showing consideration for the people who live and work in the countryside and for the wildlife that is dependent upon it. We can help by joining one of the voluntary bodies working for conservation – their names and addresses will be found in the leaflet "Who Does What for Scotland's Countryside?" published by the Countryside Commission for Scotland. And we can help by getting to know more about Scotland's scenic and historic heritage so that we become increasingly aware that it is indeed a heritage worth cherishing.

The book, Scotland's Countryside, is designed to help you do just this. In it you will find details of a great many places where you will be made welcome to the Scottish countryside and where you will be given the opportunity to discover more about it.

ADDRESSES OF THE ORGANISATIONS REFERRED TO IN THE TEXT

Countryside Commission for Scotland
Battleby, Redgorton, Perth PH1 3EW.

Forestry Commission (Scottish Headquarters)
Drumsheugh Gardens, Edinburgh EH3 7RS.

Nature Conservancy Council (Scottish Headquarters)
12 Hope Terrace, Edinburgh EH9 2AS.

National Trust for Scotland
5 Charlotte Square, Edinburgh EH2 4DU.

Royal Society for the Protection of Birds (Scottish Office)
17 Regent Terrace, Edinburgh EH7 5BN.

Scottish Wildlife Trust
8 Dublin Street, Edinburgh EH1 3PP.

Scottish Rights of Way Society Ltd.
32 Rutland Square, Edinburgh EH1 2BW.

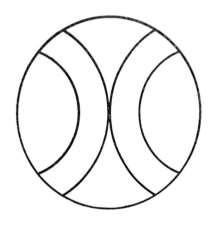

PLACES OF SCENIC AND HISTORIC INTEREST IN SCOTLAND'S COUNTRYSIDE

HOW TO FIND THE INFORMATION YOU REQUIRE

This section contains a selection of places, covering a wide range of opportunities for countryside recreation. It makes no claim to be comprehensive, but rather attempts to suggest something for every taste. Whilst every care has been taken to check the accuracy of the information given, the Countryside Commission for Scotland cannot accept responsibility for errors or omissions.

The places are arranged in alphabetical order – of counties, towns/villages and sites (with islands treated separately from the mainland). Each has a county index number which is used again in the atlas section, enabling you to locate the entries on the maps. The relevant map numbers for each county are shown at the top of the page.

The Symbols in the left-hand margin indicate the particular interest of each site. The symbols used (see key below) are among those recently introduced for use in relation to countryside recreation and are likely to become increasingly familiar in the next few years.

✝ Abbey, Cathedral or Church	𝒊 Information
𝔪 Ancient Monument	Nature Reserve
Arboretum	☆ Other Natural Attractions
Battle Site	Picnic Site
Castle	Trails and Walks
Garden	Viewpoint
Historic Property	Wildlife Park

One additional symbol ★ is used to indicate Museums of Country Life.

The organisations responsible for day-to-day care and administration of the sites are indicated opposite the site name. The abbreviations used are:—

DAFS :	Department of Agriculture and Fisheries for Scotland
FC :	Forestry Commission
NCC :	Nature Conservancy Council
NOSHEB :	North of Scotland Hydro Electric Board
NTS :	National Trust for Scotland
PSA :	Property Services Agency, Scotland, on behalf of the Secretary of State for Scotland.
RSPB :	Royal Society for the Protection of Birds.
SWT :	Scottish Wildlife Trust

Admission times are in some cases described as "standard". This term implies that hours of opening are

April–September	weekdays	9.30–7.00
	Sundays	2.00–7.00
October–March	weekdays	9.30–4.00
	Sundays	2.00–4.00

The **admission charges** given were correct at the time of going to press but rising costs may have resulted in subsequent increases.

ABERDEENSHIRE Maps 9 & 10

Ab. Aberdeen, HAZLEHEAD NATURE TRAILS　　　　*(Aberdeen Corporation)*
These trails in one of Aberdeen's Public Parks identify the plants and trees.
The booklet incorporates a short questionnaire which encourages children to
look, draw and ask questions.
Booklet (free) on site and from Parks and Recreation Dept, St Nicholas House.

Aberdeen, KIRKHILL FOREST WALKS　　　　　　　　　　*(F.C.)*
A complex of forest walks has been laid out in attractive Kirkhill Forest,
only 5 miles west of Aberdeen. Starting points of the walks can all be found
at FC car parks between the A93 and A94.

Aberdeen, LOIRSTON PARK
This proposed country park, still at the development stage, is in open country
to the south of Aberdeen.

Ab.1. Alford, CRAIGIEVAR CASTLE　　　　　　　　　　*(N.T.S.)*
Craigievar, completed in 1626, is one of the most noble and notable of the
Castles of Mar in which Scottish baronial architecture reached its greatest
heights. As with Crathes, one of the great glories of Craigievar is the
embellishment around the roof-line. Inside, Craigievar reveals magnificent
examples of richly moulded plaster ceilings.
Situation. On Lumphanan-Alford road. O.S. 1" map sheet 39, ref.
NJ 566096.
Admission.　May-Sept Wed, Thurs, Sun 2-7, also Sat 2-7 during July and
August. Oct. 1-13, Wed, Thurs, and Sun 2-6, adults 35p, children 10p.
School parties: teachers 10p, pupils 5p. Car park 10p. Guidebook 20p.

Ab.2. Alford, GLENBUCHAT CASTLE　　　　　　　　　　*(P.S.A.)*
An ancient seat of the Gordons, on upper Donside. It was built in 1590,
and is a fine example of a Z-plan castle.
Situation. 14 miles west of Alford on Cambus o' May road. O.S. 1" map
sheet 39, ref. NJ 398149.
Admission. Not yet open to the public. May be viewed from outside.
Official Guide Book for Kildrummy and Glenbuchat 14p. On sale at
Kildrummy.

Ab.3. Alford, KILDRUMMY CASTLE　　　　　　　　　　*(P.S.A.)*
The most complete example in Scotland of a secular building dating from
the 13th century.
Situation. 10 miles west of Alford on Cambus o' May road. O.S. 1" map
sheet 39, ref NJ 455164.
Admission. All times without charge. Official Guide Book for Kildrummy
and Glenbuchat 14p.

Ab.4. Auchindoir, ST MARY'S CHURCH　　　　　　　　*(P.S.A.)*
One of the finest medieval parish churches remaining in Scotland. It has
a beautiful early 16th century sacrament house.
Situation. ½ mile west of main Aberdeen-Huntly road between Lumsden
and Rhynie. O.S. 1" map sheet 39, ref NJ 477246.
Admission. All times without charge.

Ab.5. Ballater, SUMMIT OF GLENGAIRN VIEWPOINT　　*(Aberdeen C.C.)*
Hilltop picnic site at highest point on A939 road between Ballater and
Strathdon.

Ab.6. Braemar, GLENMUICK PICNIC SITE   *(Aberdeen C.C.)*
Picnic area near Loch Muick with access to Lochnagar.

Ab.7. Balmoral, CASTLE   *(Her Majesty the Queen)*
The Highland residence of Her Majesty the Queen on Deeside. The original
castle was first mentioned in 1484. Queen Victoria's first visit in 1848 was
followed by purchase of lands by the Prince Consort in 1852. The Castle was
re-built in the present Scottish Baronial style in 1855.
Situation. 50 miles from Aberdeen. A93.
Admission. Grounds only open to public during May, June and July, daily
except Sundays, 10-5. (The grounds are not open when members of the
Royal Family are in residence.) 12 p which is donated to charities.
Information on the Estate, which includes Lochnagar, Broad Cairn and
Loch Muick, can be obtained from the Estate Ranger at Linn Cottage, Birkhall,
Ballater, Aberdeenshire (Tel. Ballater 315), or from the Estates Office,
Balmoral Castle, Ballater, Aberdeenshire (Tel. Crathie 334).

Ab.8. Bennachie, BOGHEAD PICNIC SITE   *(Aberdeen C.C.)*
Near Maiden Castle on a minor road which branches off the Oyne-Chapel of
Garioch road near the Maiden Stone. Access to Bennachie footpath.

BENNACHIE FOREST WALKS   *(F.C.)*
The Back o' Bennachie Forest walks range from a short one which passes
through young mixed forestry plantations to longer walks to Oxencraig and
Mither Tap for fine views of the Buchan plain and the lower Grampians.
Situation: 1½ miles south of A979, 8 miles west of Inverurie. O.S. 1" map
sheet 40, ref NJ 662246

Bennachie MAIDEN STONE   *(P.S.A.)*
This famous Early Christian monument is associated with several weird legends.
On one side it displays a Celtic cross and on the other side are Pictish symbols.
Situation. Near Chapel of Garioch, 4½ miles north-west of Inverurie
(by Drumdurno Farm). O.S. 1" map sheet 40, ref. NJ 703247.
Admission. All times without charge.

Bennachie, WOODS OF LOGIE PICNIC SITE   *(Aberdeen C.C.)*
Woodland picnic area beside A96 road, about 1½ miles west of Pitcaple,
with information boards.

CAENLOCHAN (see Angus)

CAIRNGORMS (see Inverness-shire)

Ab.9. Cock Bridge, CORGARFF CASTLE   *(P.S.A.)*
A 16th century tower house, converted into a garrison post and enclosed
within a star-shaped loopholed wall in 1748.
Situation. ½ mile south-west of Cock Bridge. O.S. 1" map sheet 38,
ref. NJ 255086.
Admission. May be viewed from outside. Leaflet.

Ab.10.   Daviot, LOANHEAD STONE CIRCLE   *(P.S.A.)*

The best known of a group of recumbent stone circles in east Scotland
(*c.* 1800-1600 B.C.).
*Situation. ¼ mile north-west of Daviot, 5 miles north-north-west of Inverurie.
O.S. 1" map sheet 40, ref. NJ 748288.*
Admission. All times without charge.

FORESTS IN THE NORTH EAST   *(F.C.)*

Many of the great forests of the North East, owned by the Forestry Commission,
include some of the loveliest Scottish woodlands with Scots pine, European
larch and Norway spruce and many other species including less usual conifers,
the great and noble silver firs, Western red cedar and Western hemlock.
Birds include coal tits, goldcrests, mistle thrush, and siskin. Vegetation
includes chickweed wintergreen and twinflower. Forests include Bennachie,
near Inverurie; Mearns, near Stonehaven; Kirkhill, near Aberdeen; and Laigh of
Moray, near Elgin.
*Booklet, "Forests of North East Scotland" (reprinting). Forestry Commission,
6 Queen's Gate, Aberdeen AB9 2NQ.*

In the Blackhall section of Banchory Forest, two trails guide the visitor to
scenic view points, identifying the trees and wildlife while telling much of the
forester's story.
Booklet 5p from Forestry Commission, 6 Queens Gate, Aberdeen AB9 2NQ.

Ab.11.   Fraserburgh, MEMSIE BURIAL CAIRN   *(P.S.A.)*

A fine example of a large stone-built cairn (probably dating to *c.* 1500 B.C.).
*Situation. Near the village of Memsie, 3 miles south-south-west of
Fraserburgh. O.S. 1" map sheet 31, ref. NJ 977621.*
Admission. All times without charge.

Ab.12.   Garlogie, CULLERLIE STONE CIRCLE   *(P.S.A.)*

A circle of eight undressed boulders enclosing an area consecrated by fires
on which eight small cairns were later constructed (probably *c.* 2000 B.C.).
*Situation. 1 mile south of Garlogie, on Aberdeen-Echt road. O.S. 1" map
sheet 40, ref. NJ 785043.*
Admission. All times without charge.

Ab.13.   Huntly, CASTLE   *(P.S.A.)*

The remains include the foundations of a 15th century tower-house, destroyed
in 1594, and an imposing hall-house with elaborate heraldic enrichments.
Situation. ½ mile north of Huntly. O.S. 1" map sheet 30, ref. NJ 532407.
Admission. Standard. 5p. Official Guide Book 14p.

Ab.14.   Insch, PICARDY STONE   *(P.S.A.)*

A Pictish symbol stone of the oldest class, with incised symbols.
*Situation. Near Myreton, 2 miles north-west of Insch. O.S. 1" map sheet
39, ref. NJ 610303.*
Admission. All times without charge.

Ab.15.   Inverurie, BRANDSBUTT STONE   *(P.S.A.)*

A Pictish symbol stone, with a well-preserved ogham inscription; originally
one of a circle.
Situation. At Brandsbutt Farm. O.S. 1" map sheet 40, ref. NJ 760224.
Admission. All times without charge.

Ab.16. Inverurie, EAST AQUHORTHIES STONE CIRCLE *(P.S.A.)*

One of a group of Bronze Age stone circles of a type found mainly in this part of Scotland (*c.* 1800-1600 B.C.).
Situation. 2½ miles west of Inverurie. O.S. 1" map sheet 40, ref. NJ 733208.
Admission. All times without charge.

Ab.17. Inverurie, KINKELL CHURCH *(P.S.A.)*

The ruins of an early 16th century parish church, with some ornate details, including a rich sacrament house of unusual design, dated 1524.
Situation. On the Don, 2 miles south-south-east of Inverurie. O.S. 1" map sheet 40, ref. NJ 786191.
Admission. All times without charge.

Ab.18. Kennethmont, LEITH HALL *(N.T.S.)*

The earliest part of this attractive old country house dates from 1650. Additions and improvements were made in the 18th century and again during the reign of Queen Victoria, completing the hollow square plan. The family tradition of military service is reflected in the collection of personal possessions of successive lairds. The garden at Leith Hall has the same intimate charm as the house and its contents, with the rock garden and zig-zag herbaceous border as particularly attractive features.
Situation. South of Aberdeen-Huntly road. O.S. 1" map sheet 39, ref. NJ 541298.
Admission. House open May-Sept 11-1 and 2-6. Sundays 2-6. Gardens all year 10-dusk. House and garden 30p, children 10p. House 25p, children 5p. Gardens 10p, children 5p. School parties: teachers 10p, pupils 5p. Car park free.

Ab.19. Lumphanan, PEEL RING OF LUMPHANAN *(P.S.A.)*

Major early medieval earthwork, consisting of a large oval motte or mound defended by a wet ditch. Masonry foundations can be traced on the summit.
Situation. ½ mile south-west of Lumphanan. O.S. 1" map sheet 39 ref. NJ 577037.
Admission. All times without charge.

Ab.20. Newburgh, SANDS OF FORVIE NATURE RESERVE *(N.C.C.)*

North of mouth of River Ythan near Newburgh. Least disturbed large sand dune system in Scotland. Large mobile dunes and unusual communities of heathland plants on fixed dunes. Largest breeding concentration of eider duck in UK. Four species of terns, kittiwakes, fulmars, shelduck breed. Waders, ducks, geese in autumn and winter. Access by indicated paths.
Extensive research on reserve by Aberdeen University from Culterty Field Station, Newburgh. Honorary Warden: F. C. Coull, Ythan Cottage, Newburgh. Assistant Regional Officer: Nature Conservancy Council, Brathens, Banchory, Kincardineshire. Tel. 2201-5.

Newburgh, WATERSIDE PICNIC SITE *(Aberdeen C.C.)*

Picnic area beside the A975 road, overlooking the River Ythan, about 2 miles north of Newburgh.

Ab.21. Old Deer, DEER ABBEY *(P.S.A.)*

The remains of a Cistercian monastery founded in 1219. Its predecessor, the
Celtic Abbey associated with the famous Book of Deer, was on another site.
Situation. Near Old Deer. O.S. 1" map sheet 31, ref. NJ 969481.
Admission. April-September standard, but notice posted when keyholder
absent. Closed in winter. 5p. Official Guide Pamphlet 2½p.

Ab.22. Strichen, FOREST OF DEER FOREST WALKS *(F.C.)*

White Cow Wood forest walk passes through attractive open woodland and
has a badger sett viewpoint.
Situation. 2½ miles south-east of Strichen. O.S. 1" map sheet 31, ref.
NJ 957513.
Delgaty Wood forest walk goes through young mixed plantations near the Mill
of Delgaty.
Situation. 2 miles west of Turriff. O.S. 1" map sheet 30, ref NJ 758497.

Ab.23. Tarland, CULSH EARTH-HOUSE *(P.S.A.)*

A well preserved example of an earth-house with roofing slabs intact over
large chamber and entrance; of Iron Age date.
Situation. At Culsh Farm. O.S. 1" map sheet 39, ref NJ 505055.
Admission. All times without charge.

Tarland, TOMNAVERIE STONE CIRCLE *(P.S.A.)*

The remains of a recumbent stone circle (probably *c.* 1800-1600 B.C.).
Situation. Near Mill of Wester Coull, about 4 miles north-west of Aboyne
and 1 mile south-east of Tarland. O.S. 1" map sheet 39, ref. NJ 488035.
Admission. All times without charge.

Ab.24. Tarves, TARVES MEDIEVAL TOMB *(P.S.A.)*

A fine altar-tomb of William Forbes, the laird who enlarged Tolquhon Castle.
It shows an interesting mixture of Gothic and Renaissance styles.
Situation. In the kirkyard of Tarves, 4 miles north-east of Oldmeldrum.
O.S. 1" map sheet 40, ref. NJ 869312.
Admission. All times without charge.

Tarves, TOLQUHON CASTLE *(P.S.A.)*

This mansion illustrates the great advance in domestic planning during the
reign of James VI. Notable features are the gatehouse and the ornate
gun-loops.
Situation. 15 miles north-north-east of Aberdeen off the Pitmedden-
Tarves road. O.S. 1" map sheet 40, ref. NJ 874286.
Admission. Standard. 5p. Official Guide Pamphlet 2½p.

Ab.25. Udny, PITMEDDEN GARDEN *(N.T.S.)*

At Pitmedden the National Trust for Scotland has re-created the 17th century
"Great Garden" originally laid out by Sir Alexander Seton, the first baronet
of Pitmedden. Three of the formal patterns, outlined in the box hedging and
decorated annually with bedding plants, are taken from designs used in the
Gardens of Holyroodhouse, Edinburgh in 1647. The fourth of the great parterres is a
heraldic design based on Sir Alexander Seton's coat of arms. Two other
prominent features are the thunder houses at either end of the west wall.
Situation. Near Pitmedden, O.S. 1" map sheet 40, ref. NJ 885281.
Admission. Garden only open daily 9.30-dusk. Adults 20p from August-mid-
September; 15p other times. Tearoom in summer, (closed on Fridays).
Car park free. Guidebook 20p.

ANGUS

Maps 5, 9 & 10

An.1.   Arbroath, ARBROATH CLIFFS NATURE TRAIL   *(S.W.T.)*
This trail provides a comprehensive guide to the wildlife and geology of the
sea cliffs and seashore north of Arbroath.
Booklet 15p (plus postage) from Arbroath bookshops and SWT.

Arbroath, ST VIGEANS MUSEUM   *(P.S.A.)*
These Pictish gravestones form one of the most important groups of early
Christian sculpture in Scotland.
*Situation. In the village of St. Vigeans, 1½ miles north of the centre of
Arbroath. O.S. 1" map sheet 50, ref. NO 639429.
Admission. Standard, but closed on Sundays. Notice posted when
keyholder is absent. 5p. Official Guide Book, "Early Christian and Pictish
Monuments of Scotland", 25p.*

An.2.   Brechin, THE CATERTHUNS   *(P.S.A.)*
The Brown Caterthun. An excellent example of Iron Age hill fort with
four concentric ramparts and ditches interrupted by entrances and causeways.
The White Caterthun. A well-preserved hill fort of the Iron Age with
massive stone rampart and outer earthworks.
*Situation. Near the village of Menmuir, about 5 miles north-west of Brechin.
O.S. 1" map sheet 50, ref. NO 555668 and 548660.
Admission. All times without charge.*

An.3.   CAENLOCHLAN NATURE RESERVE   *(N.C.C.)*
An extensive mountain reserve, lying between Glen Clova and Glas Maol,
which is of great biological and geological interest. Authority is required to
visit the Reserve in late summer and autumn.

An.4.   Dundee, CAMPERDOWN PARK   *(City of Dundee)*
Over 600 acres of parkland with ornamental trees, nature trails and study
centre, children's zoo, wildfowl ponds. Leaflet from Parks and Recreation
Department, 17 City Square, Dundee and children's zoo. Nature trail booklet
10p.   Tel. 0382 23141.
Situation. Kingsway West/Coupar Angus Road.

An.5.   Eassie, SCULPTURED STONE   *(P.S.A.)*
A fine example of an elaborately sculptured Early Christian monument.
*Situation. In the old churchyard of Eassie off the Glamis-Meigle road.
O.S. 1" map sheet 50, ref. NO 353475.
Admission. All times without charge.*

An.6.   Edzell, CASTLE   *(P.S.A.)*
This was the finest castle in Angus. The garden wall exhibits a display of
heraldic and symbolical decoration unique in Britain.
*Situation. 1 mile west of Edzell, 5 miles north of Brechin. O.S. 1" map
sheet 50, ref. NO 585691.
Admission. Standard. 5p. Official Guide Book 11p.*

An.7.   Edzell, GLENESK MUSEUM   *(The Glenesk Trust)*
The museum shows Glen life in general. This is an authentic re-creation
chiefly of the immediate past, but also covers such subjects as the
archaeology, geology and wildlife of the district. Exhibits include relics of
farming, trades, sport, domestic scenes with costumes, music and children's
rooms. In the same building (The Retreat), past meets present. The Trust

provides a tearoom and home produce stall, while a highland home industries shop has a large selection of Scottish crafts for sale.
Situation. 10 miles from Edzell on Glenesk road.
Admission 12p, children 5p. Open Easter weekend and Sundays from Easter, then daily June 1 to September 30 (inclusive) 2-6. Evening parties catered for. Conducted tours for school parties morning and afternoon by arrangement from April onwards. Tel. Tarfside 236 (Museum), Tarfside 254 (Tearoom).

An.8. Forfar, ABERLEMNO SCULPTURED STONES (P.S.A.)
A splendid upright cross-slab, with Pictish symbols and figure sculpture on the reverse, in Aberlemno kirkyard, and three stones beside the road (B9134).
Situation. 5 miles north-east of Forfar. O.S. map sheet 50, ref. NO 523555 and 523559.
Admission. All times without charge.

An.9. Forfar, RESTENNETH PRIORY (P.S.A.)
A house of Augustinian canons regular, probably founded by David I.
A feature of the ruins is the tall square tower, with its shapely broach spire.
Situation. 1½ miles east of Forfar. O.S. 1" map sheet 50, ref. NO 482516.
Admission. All reasonable times without charge. Official Guide Book 9p.

An.10. Glamis, KIRKWYND COTTAGES (N.T.S.)
This neat row of cottages, full of local character, is now the home of the Angus Folk Collection covering domestic and agricultural life in the county in the 19th century and earlier. The cottages were built in the 17th century and restored by the National Trust for Scotland.
Situation. In Glamis. O.S. 1" map sheet 50, ref. NO 386468.
Admission. Open Easter to end of September, daily 1-6; and on request to caretaker (Mrs J. Irons) in village. Adults 15p, children 5p.

An.11. Kirriemuir, BARRIE'S BIRTHPLACE (N.T.S.)
Sir James M. Barrie's birth-place, No 9 Brechin Road, is now maintained by the Trust as an intimate personal museum of Barrie's achievement in the world of letters. It contains sections of original manuscripts, personal possessions of the writer and mementos of actors and producers associated with his plays.
Situation. In Kirriemuir. O.S. 1" map sheet 50, ref. NO 388541.
Admission. Open: April-October, weekdays 10-12.30, 2-6; Sunday 2-6. Other times by arrangement 10p. Children accompanied by adults free. Guidebook 10p. Tel. Kirriemuir 2646
Nearby (not in the Trust's care) are the Auld Licht Manse and the Window in Thrums.

An.12. Kirriemuir, LOCH OF LINTRATHEN NATURE RESERVE (S.W.T.)
Loch with flocks of wintering wildfowl, including wigeon, mallard, tufted duck and greylag geese. Observation hide at Balnakeilly on west side of loch is the only point at which public access is permitted.
Situation. Car park is on minor road leaving B951 at north-west corner of loch.
Admission. Hide open at weekends only, 2-dusk.

An.13. Monifieth, ARDESTIE AND CARLUNGIE EARTH-HOUSES (P.S.A.)
Two examples of large earth-houses attached to surface dwellings used in first centuries A.D.
Situation. About 7 miles east of Dundee north of Arbroath road.
O.S. 1" map sheet 50, ref. NO 502344 and 511359.
Admission. All times without charge.

An.14. Monikie, AFFLECK CASTLE *(P.S.A.)*

A late 15th century tower-house on the L-plan, still in perfect condition. The solar, or upper hall, is a room of exceptional distinction.

Situation. 8 miles north-east of Dundee. O.S. 1" map sheet 50, ref. NO 495388.

Admission. All reasonable times, except Sundays, on application to custodian, but notice posted when he is absent. 5p. Official Guide Pamphlet 1p.

ST CYRUS (see Kincardineshire)

An.15. Tealing, EARTH-HOUSE *(P.S.A.)*

A well preserved example of an Iron Age souterrain or earth-house comprising a passage and long curved gallery and small inner chamber.

Situation. 5 miles north of Dundee off Dundee-Forfar road. O.S. 1" map sheet 50, ref. NO 413382.

Admission. All times without charge.

ARGYLL

Ar.1. ARGYLL FOREST PARK *(F.C.)*

The Argyll Forest Park lies on the Cowal Peninsula, between Loch Long and Loch Fyne. Though it is close to the industrial zone of mid-Scotland, it is a region altogether different in character and scenery. Here rugged bens, their foothills clad in green woods of spruce and pine, soar from the shores of sea lochs to heights above 3,000 feet. Its lower levels carry a few good roads and several fascinating footpaths; its summits attract the rock climber. This park holds 60,000 acres in the three forests of Ardgartan, Glenbranter and Benmore. It is so broken up by peaks and lochs that it can only be approached by one of two routes; these are linked by a good road, but not by through public transport. At Ardgartan is the main camping site, well-placed on a promontory jutting out into the sea. Above it rise the well-known climbing grounds of the Cobbler (2,891 feet) and the higher neighbouring peaks of Beinn Narnain (3,036 feet) and Beinn Ime (3,318 feet). Beyond Ardgartan, the main road climbs the famous Rest-and-be-Thankful pass. Near Benmore is a public path, leading to viewpoints, which follows a deep cleft in the hills known as Puck's Glen. On the east side of the Holy Loch, close to Kilmun Church stands a Forest Garden holding plots of many unusual trees.

Booklet, "Argyll Forest Park Guide" 35p (F.C.). Guide "Kilmun Arboretum and Forest Plots" 10p (F.C.). Warden, Camp Site, Ardgartan, Arrochar and Forest Office, Kilmun, near Dunoon.

Other booklets of local interest, including forest walks, published by Dunoon and Cowal Tourist Organisation.

BEN LUI (See Perthshire)

Ar.2. Benmore, YOUNGER BOTANIC GARDEN *(D.A.F.S.)*

Extensive woodland gardens featuring conifers, rhododendrons, azaleas and many other shrubs.

Situation. 7 miles north-west of Dunoon on Strachur road.

Admission. Open daily April to September 10-6. Adults 10p, children and O.A.P.'s 5p. Guidebook. Tearoom (see also Argyll Forest Park).

Ar.3. Bonawe, ARDCHATTAN PRIORY *(P.S.A.)*

One of the three Valliscaulian houses founded in Scotland in 1230. The remains include several monuments in the characteristic late West Highland style.

Situation. On the north side of Loch Etive, 7 miles north-east of Oban. O.S. 1" map sheet 46, ref. NM 971349.

Admission. All times without charge.

Ar.4. Connel Bridge, BARCALDINE FOREST WALKS *(F.C.)*

Set amid spectacular Highland scenery, two walks, Glen Dubh and Eas na Circe, wind through Barcaldine Forest above Loch Creran with fine views of the hills to the west.

Situation. On A828 6 miles north of Connel Bridge. Enquiries to Forest Office, Barcaldine.

Ar.5. Corran Ferry, DOIRE DONN NATURE RESERVE *(S.W.T.)*

Regenerating natural oakwood on north-west shore of Loch Linnhe. Permit required — obtainable from Secretary, 8 Dublin Street, Edinburgh EH1 3PP.

Situation. 7 miles north-east of Corran Ferry on Mallaig road.

Ar.6. Dalmally, CRUACHAN DAM AND TUNNEL (N.O.S.H.E.B.)

From the Reception Centre beside Loch Awe visits can be made to the dam and St Conan's Kirk and into the cavern under the mountain. Special arrangements can be made for pre-booked parties and a 15 minute film "The Hollow Mountain" is available for showing to educational groups.

Ar.7. Dunoon, KILMUN ARBORETUM AND FOREST PLOTS (F.C.)

Managed by Forestry Commission research staff, the Arboretum contains forest trees from many parts of the world grown for study purposes. In addition to Scotland's finest collection of Australian eucalyptus, there are Dawn redwoods from China, Southern beech from Chile and a wide variety of ornamental trees and flowering shrubs. Three recommended walks offer routes of varying duration.
Admission. Free. Open to the public from sunrise to sunset.
Leaflet, 10p, from Forest Office, Kilmun, near Dunoon.

Ar.8. GLENCOE (N.T.S.)

Some of the finest climbing and walking country in the Highlands is included in the 14,200 acres owned by the National Trust for Scotland in Glencoe and Dalness. Like all of the Trust's outdoor properties it is accessible to the public at all times. Good intelligence on details of routes, timings and weather prospects can be had at the Trust's information office at the Clachaig layby in Glencoe. The main scene of the massacre of 1692 is now the site of the village and is not included in National Trust for Scotland property.
Guidebook 10p (NTS), NTS Information Centre at Clachaig lay-by, open mid-May to mid-October 10-6, Sunday 2-6. Warden: Mr Duncan MacColl, Ranger-Naturalist, Mr James Strachan, Guided Walks Programme.

Glencoe, FOREST WALKS (F.C.)

The Signal Rock Trail, 1½ miles, recalls the Glencoe Massacre in 1692, while the Lochan Nature Trail, 2 miles, identifies many of the exotic trees that have been planted in the area. Caravan and camp site on A82 1 mile east of Glencoe village.
Booklet 10p from Head Forester, Glencoe; Camp Warden.

Ar.9. Inveraray, AUCHINDRAIN MUSEUM OF FARMING LIFE
(Auchindrain Museum Trust)

A cluster of 18th and 19th century houses and farm buildings preserved amid their fields and furnished with farm tools and household equipment collected locally and from the site itself, illustrating life on a multiple-tenancy farm.
Situation. 6 miles south-west of Inveraray. O.S. 1" map sheet 53, ref. NN 031032.
Admission. Open daily 10-6, Sundays 2-6. 20p, Children 5p.
Cars free. Refreshments, craft products. Guides and Resident Custodian. About 1 hour needed to visit all displays. Car park with adjacent Information Centre. Tel. Furnace 235.

Ar. 10. Inveraray, CRARAE FOREST GARDEN (F.C.)

This attractive forest garden is open to the public during daylight hours throughout the year. Covering thirty-three acres, the garden comprises a collection of 107 plots of conifers, principally spruces, firs and hemlocks, and specimen trees of many rare or unusual species, both coniferous and broadleaved.
Situation. 3 miles south-west of Furnace on the Lochgilphead road. Access is obtained beside the gardens of Crarae House.

Ar.11.   Kilberry, SCULPTURED STONES   *(P.S.A.)*

A collection of late medieval sculptured stones from the Kilberry estate.
*Situation. Kilberry Castle, 17 miles south-south-west of Lochgilphead on
the west coast of Knapdale. O.S. 1" map sheet 58, ref NR 710643.*
Admission. All times without charge.

Ar.12.   Kilmartin, RELICS   *(P.S.A.)*

Both prehistoric and medieval relics can be seen in this area. The most
notable are:
(a) Bronze Age cup-and-ring engravings at Ballygowan (NR 820974) and
Baluachraig (NR 832971).
(b) Bronze Age and earlier burial cairns at Dunchraigaig (NR 833968),
Nether Largie (NR 832985, 831984 and 829980), Ri Cruin (NR 825972)
and Kilmartin Glebe (NR 833989).
(c) A stone circle (dating probably from *c.* 2000 B.C.) at Temple Wood
(NR 826979).
(d) Sculptured stones and crosses, dating from the 16th century in Kilmartin
Churchyard (NR 835988).
Admission. All times without charge. O.S. 1" map sheet 52.

Ar.13.   Kilmory Knap, CHAPEL   *(P.S.A.)*

A typical small church of the West Highlands, unicameral and with a pair
of round arched east windows. There are sculptured stones in the chapel.
Situation. In South Knapdale. O.S. 1" map sheet 58, ref. NR 703753.
Admission. All times without charge.

Ar.14.   Kintyre, CARRADALE FOREST WALKS AND FOREST CENTRE *(F.C.)*

Several walks of varying length offer changing views of forest, hills and sea.
Viewpoints overlook the Kilbrennan Sound to Arran and Carradale River and
Glen.
Situation. 1 mile south of Dippen off B842 Campbeltown to Tarbert Road.

Ar.15.   Loch Awe, NATURE TRAIL AND FOREST WALKS   *(F.C.)*

The booklet covers one forest trail and nine forest walks in Inverliever Forest.
The trail ($2\frac{1}{4}$ miles) identifies much of the forest wildlife while the pleasant walks
vary from $1\frac{1}{4}$ miles to 5 miles.
*Situation. On the west shore of Loch Awe, about 15 miles south of
Taynuilt on B845.*
Booklet 15p from Chief Forester, Inverliever Forest, by Taynuilt, Argyll.

Ar.16.   Loch Awe, KILCHURN CASTLE   *(P.S.A.)*

This 15th century castle stands prominently in a marsh at the end of
Loch Awe in a situation of great natural beauty.
*Situation. 2 miles west of Dalmally; clearly visible from the main road.
O.S. map sheet 53, ref. NN 133276.*
Admission. Not open to the public. May be viewed from outside.

Ar.17.   Lochgilphead, CUP-AND-RING ENGRAVINGS   *(P.S.A.)*

Engravings (dating from *c.* 2000-1500 B.C.) occur on rock outcrops at
Achnabreck (NR 856906), Cairnbaan (NR 838910) and Kilmichael Glassary
(NR 858935).

27

Lochgilphead, DUNADD FORT *(P.S.A.)*

A well preserved Dark Age hill-fort with walled enclosures, identified as
the capital of Dalriada, the Kingdom of the Scots.
*Situation. 1½ miles west of Kilmichael Glassary, off Lochgilphead-Kilmartin
road. O.S. 1" map sheet 52, ref. NR 837936.*
Admission. All times without charge.

Lochgilphead, KNAPDALE FOREST CENTRE AND WALKS *(F.C.)*

A log cabin in the forest serves as a small information centre covering all
aspects of Knapdale Forest. The walks in the Knapdale-Crinan area cater for
wide interests — wildlife, local history and archaeology and fish management.
*Situation. Near junction of road from Lochgilphead to Tayvallich and
Achnamara. Full details of forest walks from Guide, 10p, obtainable from
Forest Centre.*

Ar.18.   Oban, DUNSTAFFNAGE CASTLE *(P.S.A.)*

An exceptionally fine and well preserved example of a 13th century castle
of enceinte, showing the usual great curtain wall and round towers.
*Situation. On the south shore of Loch Etive, 3 miles north-north-east
of Oban. O.S. 1" map sheet 46, ref. NM 883345.*
Admission. Closed to the public. May be viewed from the outside only.

Ar.19.   Strontian, ARIUNDLE OAKWOOD *(N.C.C. & D.A.F.S.)*

Native oak woodlands with rich associations of bryophytes.

Strontian, STRONTIAN GLEN NATURE TRAIL

Strontian Glen Nature Trail, following the right bank of the Strontian river,
passes through Ariundle Oakwood to high moorland with disused leadmines.
The varied plant and animal life is described in the *booklet (3p) available from
Strontian Village Centre and Nature Conservancy Council, Hon. Warden,
Mr R. Cameron, Strathview, Strontian.*

Ar.20.   Taynuilt, GLEN NANT *(F.C. & N.C.C.)*

This is a fine example of natural mixed-deciduous woodland of ash, hazel,
oak and birch. Permission required to visit.
Situation. 1 mile south of Taynuilt, on Kilchrenan road.

Ar.21.   Tayvallich, CASTLE SWEEN *(P.S.A.)*

This lonely ruin appears to be one of the earliest stone castles in Scotland.
It was probably built in the mid-12th century.
*Situation. On the east shore of Loch Sween, in South Knapdale.
O.S. 1" map sheet 58, ref. NR 713789.*
Admission. All times without charge.

Ar.22.   TIGHNABRUAICH WILDLIFE CENTRE AND FOREST TRAIL *(F.C.)*

Photo-safari hides, each holding four people, overlooking a lochan in a 9 acre
site with assorted duck, roe deer, and blue hares. Caladh Castle Forest Trail
(1½ miles) leads to viewpoints overlooking Caladh Bay and Kyles of Bute.
A folded sheet identifies much of the wildlife interest in the forest.
Situation. 2 miles north of Tighnabruaich.
Booking charge for hides 20p per person per watch.
Booklet from Forest Office, Hafton, Tighnabruaich.

Ar.23.   Easdale, EILEACH AN NAOIMH   (P.S.A.)

An island with an interesting group of Celtic monastic remains (associated
in local tradition with St Columba), including beehive cells, a chapel and
a graveyard.
*Situation. One of the Garvellach Isles, in the Firth of Lorne. O.S. 1" map
sheet 52, ref. NM 668119.*
*Admission. All times without charge; by privately hired motor boat from
Cullipool or Easdale. Enquiries to the keykeeper. Telephone: Luing 212.*

Ar.24.   Iona, MACLEAN'S CROSS   (P.S.A.)

A fine 15th century free standing cross of the Hebridean type.
*Situation. On the island of Iona, by the roadside between the village and
the abbey. O.S. 1" map sheet 51, ref. NM 284243.*
Admission. All times without charge.

Ar.25.   Mull, THE BURG   (N.T.S.)

Information at Burg farm from Miss C. McGillivray. McCulloch's fossil tree,
possibly 50 million years old, can be reached at low water. Cars inadvisable
beyond Tiroran. Walking time from Burg cottage to fossil tree is about three
hours (return trip); stout footwear needed.
*Situation. On north side of Loch Scridain, on the Ardmeonach Peninsula.
O.S. 1" map sheet 51, ref. NM 426266.*

AYRSHIRE

Ay.   Ayr, ROZELLE NATURE TRAILS *(Ayr Burgh/S.W.T.)*
The Pond Walk and the Woodland Walk, the first two of a proposed series,
describe the animal and plant life found in a stretch of woodland which
contains two ponds.
*Booklet 6p from Parks Department, 30 Miller Road, Ayr, or from the
Mansion House, Rozelle.*

Ay.1.   BALLANTRAE NATURE RESERVE *(S.W.T.)*
Shingle spit, with adjoining tidal mudflats, lagoons and meadows, of
botanical and ornithological interest. Visitors are asked to comply with
notices requesting them not to walk on marked parts of the reserve.
Situation. At the mouth of the river Stinchar, South of Ballantrae.

Ay.2.   Dalmellington, LOCH DOON CASTLE *(P.S.A.)*
This 14th century castle was transplanted some years ago from the middle
of the loch when the water level was raised. Its plan is unusual.
*Situation. 7 miles south of Dalmellington. O.S. 1" map sheet 67,
ref. NX 484950.*
Admission. All times without charge.

GALLOWAY FOREST PARK (see Kirkcudbrightshire).

Ay.3.   Kilmarnock, DUNDONALD CASTLE *(P.S.A.)*
King Robert II rebuilt this castle and died there in 1390. The large oblong
tower-house incorporates the remains of a 13th century gatehouse.
*Situation. At Dundonald, 4½ miles south-west of Kilmarnock off main road
to Troon. O.S. 1" map sheet 67, ref. NS 363345.*
Admission. Not yet open to the public. May be viewed from the outside.

Ay.4.   Kilmarnock, ROWALLAN CASTLE *(P.S.A.)*
This house is a fine specimen of a superior Scottish mansion of the
16th and 17th centuries.
*Situation. In the Rowallan estate, about 3 miles north of Kilmarnock.
O.S. 1" map sheet 60, ref NS 435424.*
Admission. Not yet open to the public. May be viewed from outside.

Ay.5.   Kirkoswald, SOUTER JOHNNIE'S HOUSE *(N.T.S.)*
This thatched and limewashed cottage was the home of the village cobbler
John Davidson at the end of the 18th century. Davidson and his friend
Douglas Graham of Shanter Farm, known to Robert Burns in his youth
in Kirkoswald, were later immortalised by the bard as Souter Johnnie and
Tam o' Shanter in his epic narrative poem. The cottage contains a varied
collection of Burnsiana, contemporary tools of the cobbler's craft; and in scale
and furnishing it remains an interesting reflection of the ways of life in
Burns' day.
Situation. In Kirkoswald, on the Maybole-Turnberry road.
*Admission. Open weekdays 2.30-8, April-September, or by arrangement.
Adult 10p, child with adult free. Guidebook 10p.*

Ay.6.   Maidens, CULZEAN CASTLE *(N.T.S.)* **AND COUNTRY PARK**
The combined attractions of castle, gardens and surrounding wooded
policies, situated on the Clyde coast have made Culzean one of the most
popular and most-visited places of interest in Scotland. An energetic family
can take the best part of a day to exploit fully the walks through the
great 565-acre pleasance around the castle. The castle itself reflects the
Georgian age of elegance in the delicate, decorative plaster work of its

ceilings, the sweep of its central staircase, and the grand gesture of its round drawingroom. It was designed by one of the most prominent 18th century architects, Robert Adam, for the 10th Earl of Cassillis. The west wing, which is not open to visitors, was added at the end of the last century. Advance bookings arranged. Tel. Kirkoswald 274. There is a Trust Information Centre. Tel. Kirkoswald 236 (Custodian: Mr J. Letham Connell).
In Culzean Country Park (administered by 3 local authorities and the N.T.S.) garden and woodland nature trails identify some of the exotic trees and shrubs. Park centre, exhibition, restaurant, shop. (Chief Ranger-Naturalist and Park Principal: Mr Douglas Bremner). Tel. Kirkoswald 269. Guided walks programme. Special arrangements for school parties.
Situation. 2 miles north of Maidens on the Ayr-Girvan road.
Admission. Castle, March-Oct. inclusive, 10-6 daily. Special arrangements outside season on request. Castle 40p (children and senior citizens 10p), parties – adults 20p, school 10p.
Culzean Country Park. *Open all year. Exhibition centre and shop, daily 10-6, March-Oct. inclusive. Restaurant: Feb.-June, daily 10-6: July-Sept. 10-8: October 10-6, or by arrangement. Ranger-Naturalist service. Admission to Park free. Cars 30p, mini-buses £1, coaches £2 (March-Oct. inclusive). Admission to Park free for vehicles at other times.*

Ay.7. Maybole, CROSSRAGUEL ABBEY (P.S.A.)
A Cluniac monastery founded in 1244. The remains of the abbey are very extensive and of high architectural distinction.
Situation. 2 miles from Maybole on the Maybole-Girvan road.
O.S. 1" map sheet 72, ref. NS 275083.
Admission. Standard 5p. Guide book 14p.

Ay.8. Maybole, COLLEGIATE CHURCH (P.S.A.)
The roofless ruin of a 15th century church, built for a small college established here in 1373 by the Kennedies of Dunure.
Situation. In Maybole, south of main road. O.S. 1" map sheet 72, ref. NS 301099.
Admission. Not yet open to the public. Visible from the street.

Ay.9. Tarbolton, BACHELORS' CLUB (N.T.S.)
In this 17th century thatched house Burns and his friends formed their club in 1780, and Burns was initiated into Freemasonry there in 1781.
Situation. In Tarbolton village, 7½ miles N.E. of Ayr (off A 758). O.S. 1" map sheet 67, ref. NS 439272.
Admission on request. Key with Custodian, Mr Samuel Hay, 28 Croft Street, Tarbolton (Tel. 424),

Ay.10. Tarbolton, ENTERKINE WOOD NATURE RESERVE (S.W.T.)
Natural woodland with badgers' setts, pond and varied birdlife and a nature trail, off road to Annbank. The nature trail through the wood emphasises the changing habitat and the need for conservation. Non-members of Scottish Wildlife Trust require permits, except on open days when members of the public are particularly welcomed.
Hon Warden, Mr J. Lorrain-Smith, Auchenbeg Crescent, Ayr. Permit and trail booklet (5p) from Warden.
Limited reception facilities; parties who wish to visit the reserve should book with the Warden or Branch Secretary.

ISLANDS
Ay.11. HORSE ISLAND NATURE RESERVE (R.S.P.B.)
A low rocky island with sandy bays. Five species of gull nest, also terns, eider, oystercatcher and rock pipit.
Access. By permit only from the RSPB Scottish Office, 17 Regent Terrace, Edinburgh, EH7 5BN.

BANFF

Ba.1. Banff, DUFF HOUSE   *(P.S.A.)*

Although incomplete, William Adam's splendid and richly detailed mansion
is amongst the finest works of Georgian baroque architecture in Britain.
Situation. ½ mile south of Banff, access from bypass south of the burgh.
O.S. 1" map sheet 30, ref. NJ 692634.
Admission. Not yet open to the public. May be viewed from outside.

CAIRNGORMS (see Inverness-shire).

Ba.2. Cullen, DESKFORD CHURCH   *(P.S.A.)*

This ruined building possesses a rich sacrament house, of the type peculiar
to the north-east of Scotland during the early 16th century (c.f. Kinkell).
Situation. 4 miles south of Cullen, in Kirktown of Deskford.
O.S. 1" map sheet 30, ref. NJ 509617.
Admission. All times without charge.

Ba.3. Dufftown, AUCHINDOUN CASTLE   *(P.S.A.)*

A massive ruin on the summit of an isolated hill, enclosed by prehistoric
earthworks.
Situation. In Glen Fiddich, 2 miles south-east of Dufftown. O.S. 1" map
sheet 29, ref. NJ 349375.
Admission. Not open to the public. May be viewed from outside.

Ba.4. Dufftown, BALVENIE CASTLE   *(P.S.A.)*

This ancient stronghold of the Comyns mostly built in the 15th and
16th centuries is one of the largest and best preserved castles in the north
of Scotland.
Situation. At Dufftown. O.S. 1" map sheet 29, ref. NJ 326408.
Admission. Standard 5p. Official Guide Pamphlet 2½p.

Ba.5. Tomintoul, COUNTRY WALK AND PICNIC AREA
(Banff CC/Glenavon Estate)

This 2-mile walk starts ½ mile south of Tomintoul (cars should be left in the
village) and the picnic area is halfway along the route. Leaflet 5p available
locally.

Tomintoul, DRUMIN PICNIC SITE   *(Banff CC)*

Picnic area by B9136, about 1 mile from its junction with the B9008, near
rural craft centre.

Tomintoul, WELL OF LECHT PICNIC SITE   *(Banff CC)*

Picnic area with footpath to disused ironstone mine. On A939 road to Deeside,
5 miles from Tomintoul.

BERWICKSHIRE Maps 5 & 6

Be.1. Abbey St Bathans, EDINSHALL BROCH *(P.S.A.)*
Listed among the ten Iron Age brochs known in Lowland Scotland. Its
dimensions are exceptionally large.
*Situation. On the north-eastern slope of Cockburn Law, about 4 miles from
Grantshouse, by the Duns road. O.S. 1" map sheet 63, ref. NT 773604.
Admission. All times without charge.*

Be.2. Chirnside, FOULDEN TITHE BARN *(P.S.A.)*
A two-storeyed tithe barn with outside stair and crow-stepped
gables. Complete.
*Situation. At Foulden, 3 miles east of Chirnside, on the road to
Berwick-upon-Tweed. O.S. 1" map sheet 64, ref. NT 928556.
Admission. Not open to the public. May be viewed from the roadside.*

Be.3. DUNS CASTLE NATURE RESERVE *(S.W.T.)*
Woodland and loch with rich bird life. Marsh and swamp plants and insects.
*Permits required. Obtainable from the Warden, Mr A. Cowieson, Tottlemerrie,
Preston, Duns.*

Be.4. Duns, EDROM CHURCH *(P.S.A.)*
Of the ancient and now ruined Parish Church of Edrom, there survives a
Norman doorway of great beauty, incorporated in a burial vault.
*Situation. In Edrom, 3 miles east-north-east of Duns, off the road to
Berwick-upon-Tweed. O.S. 1" map sheet 63, ref. NT 828558.
Admission. All times without charge.*

Be.5. GORDON MOSS NATURE RESERVE *(S.W.T.)*
A wet, acid peat bog with high botanical and entomological interest.
Permits required. Obtainable from the Warden, Mr J. Waldie, West End, Gordon.

Gordon, GREENKNOWE TOWER *(P.S.A.)*
A fine turreted tower-house on the L-plan, dated 1581, and still retaining
its iron yett.
*Situation. ½ mile west of Gordon, on the Earlston road. O.S. 1" map
sheet 63 ref. NT 639428.
Admission. All reasonable times without charge on application to
custodian. Leaflet.*

Be.6. Lauder, CAMBRIDGE CROSSROADS PICNIC SITE *(Berwick C.C.)*
Picnic area beside the A697 road about 4 miles east of Lauder.

Be.7. Melrose, DRYBURGH ABBEY *(P.S.A.)*
The ruins are of high architectural interest because the claustral buildings
have survived in a more complete state than in any other Scottish monastery
except Iona and Inchcolm.
*Situation. 3 miles south-east of Melrose near St Boswells. O.S. 1" map
sheet 70 ref. NT 591317.
Admission. Standard. 10p. Official Guide Book 10p. The "Scottish Border
Abbeys Popular Guide" is also available price 10p.*

BUTESHIRE

Maps 3 & 4

ISLE OF ARRAN

Bu.1.   Blackwaterfoot, AUCHAGALLON STONE CIRCLE   *(P.S.A.)*
A Bronze Age burial cairn surrounded by a circle of fifteen standing stones.
Situation. By the east side of a farm road 4 miles north of Blackwaterfoot.
O.S. 1" map sheet 66 ref. NR 893347.
Admission. All times without charge.

Blackwaterfoot, MOSS FARM ROAD STONE CIRCLE   *(P.S.A.)*
Remains of a Bronze Age cairn and stone circle.
Situation. Signposted from A841 3 miles north of Blackwaterfoot.
Admission. All times without charge.

Bu.2.   Brodick, CASTLE, GARDENS AND GOATFELL   *(N.T.S.)*
An outstanding collection of paintings, furnishings and works of art, a superb
woodland garden, a not too arduous but rewarding hill-walk, and the
Clyde steamer trip to get there and back, make Brodick Castle a notable
expedition in countryhouse-going. The castle occupies an impressive
site overlooking Brodick Bay, one known to have been fortified in Viking
times, and is thought to include remnants of a 14th century tower associated
with Robert the Bruce. A wide variety of rare shrubs, massed azaleas, a
water garden and rose garden are notable features, while a wealth of works
of art is displayed in the Castle. Behind the castle and gardens a
well-defined path on the slopes of Goatfell leads to one of the classic summit
views of the west coast, taking in the Firth of Clyde, Ailsa Craig, Islay and the
Paps of Jura, Ben Cruachan and Ben Lomond. There is a Trust Information
Centre at the castle. A self-guided tour of the gardens and policies focuses
on the collection of exotic trees and plants.
Access by steamer from Ardrossan (summer steamer trips from Largs and
Dunoon); 1½ miles from Brodick Pier.
Admission. Castle Easter-September 1-5 daily Sundays 2-5. Gardens all
year 10-5 daily. Castle and Gardens 35p, children 15p. Gardens 20p, children 5p.
Parties: Castle and Gardens 20p, school pupils 10p (parties advised to book
in advance. Tel. Brodick 2202). Car park 10p. Guidebook 15p. Tearoom.

Bu.3.   Kilmory, CAIRN BAN   *(P.S.A.)*
One of the most famous of the Neolithic long cairns in south-west Scotland.
From the semi-circular forecourt a gallery ran into the cairn.
Situation. 3½ miles north of Kilmory on A841 and 1 mile north of
Auchareaoch Farm. O.S. 1" map sheet 66, ref. NR 991262.
Admission. All times without charge.

Kilmory, TORR A' CHAISTEAL   *(P.S.A.)*
A former headland crowned with a circular Iron Age fort now largely buried.
The entrance passage was on the east side.
Situation. 2¼ miles west of Kilmory on road A481 near Corriecravie Farm.
O.S. 1" map sheet 66, ref. NR 922233.
Admission. All times without charge.

Kilmory, TORRYLIN CAIRN   *(P.S.A.)*

A Neolithic chambered cairn in which the remains of eight skeletons, a flint
knife and part of a round-bottomed pot were found.
*Situation. South end of island, ½ mile south-west of Kilmory. O.S. 1" map
sheet 66, ref. NR 955211.*
Admission. All times without charge.

Bu.4.   Lochranza, CASTLE   *(P.S.A.)*

Remains of what is probably a 16th century building. The existence of a
castle here is first recorded at the end of the fourteenth century.
Situation. Lochranza, Arran. O.S. 1" map sheet 66, ref. NR 934507.
Access by Clyde coast steamer.
*Admission. Free on application to keykeeper, Mr T. Kerr, Post Office
Lochranza.*

ISLE OF BUTE

Bu.5.   Kingarth, ST BLANES CHURCH   *(P.S.A.)*

This well preserved monastic site, founded by a follower of St Columba, was
a place of worship and a centre of learning from the 6th until the
18th century.
Situation. South end of the island, 3 miles south of Kingarth.
O.S. 1" map sheet 59, ref. NS 094534.
Admission. Not yet open to the public. May be viewed from the outside.

Bu.6.   Rothesay, THE BUTE MUSEUM NATURE TRAILS
(Buteshire Natural History Society)

The seven Bute Nature Trails cover a range of habitats. They set out to make
the visitor more aware of the natural and local history of the areas they
describe. They include the Motorists Nature Trail which leads the car-borne
visitor on a tour of most of the island's roads, pointing out many of the sites
of archaeological and historical interest, and drawing attention to the wild life
and geology which may be seen from a car.
Leaflets 5p-10p from the Museum.

CAITHNESS

Map 13

Ca.1. Lybster, GREY CAIRNS OF CAMSTER   *(P.S.A.)*

Two megalithic chambered cairns (*c.* 3000-2000 B.C.). One cairn is elongated with expanded ends or "horns" and the other is round.

Situation. 5 miles north of Lybster, on the west side of the Lybster-Watten road. O.S. 1" map sheet 16, ref. ND 260443.
Admission. All times without charge.

Ca.2. Lybster, HILL O' MANY STANES   *(P.S.A.)*

Neolithic or Bronze Age site with almost 200 stones of no great size set out in 22 parallel rows.

Situation. 3¼ miles east-north-east of Lybster and ½ mile west of main road. O.S. 1" map sheet 11, ref. ND 295384.
Admission. All times without charge.

Ca.3. Reay, CNOC FREICEADAIN   *(P.S.A.)*

Two Neolithic long-horned cairns lying at right angles to each other on the crest of a hill.

Situation. 1 mile north of Shebster and ¼ mile west of Shebster-Achreamie road. O.S. 1" map sheet 11, ref. ND 012654.
Admission. All times without charge.

Ca.4. Thurso, ST MARY'S CHAPEL   *(P.S.A.)*

A rudely-constructed chapel, access from chancel to nave being by a low and narrow doorway with inclining jambs; probably 12th century.

Situation. ½ mile west of Crosskirk, on the coast 6 miles west of Thurso. O.S. 1" map sheet 11, ref. ND 025701.
Admission. All times without charge.

Ca.5. Wick, CAIRN OF GET   *(P.S.A.)*

A Neolithic short-horned cairn of a type found only in this part of Scotland. Excavation in 1866 revealed skeletons, arrowheads and pottery.

Situation. 6½ miles south-south-west of Wick and ½ mile west of Ulbster. O.S. 1" map sheet 16, ref. ND 314410.
Admission. All times without charge.

Ca.6. Wick, CASTLE OF OLD WICK   *(P.S.A.)*

A ruined square tower of four unvaulted storeys, standing on a spine of rock projecting into the sea; it probably dates from the 12th century.

Situation. 1 mile south of Wick on the coast half a mile east of the main road. O.S. 1" map sheet 16, ref. ND 369489.
Admission. All times without charge, except that access prohibited when adjoining rifle range in use.

CLACKMANNANSHIRE   Maps 4 & 5

Cl.1.   Clackmannan, TOWER   *(P.S.A.)*
Before the partial collapse of this castle with its 14th century tower, it was
one of the most complete of Scottish tower-houses.
*Situation. On the west side of Clackmannan. O.S. 1" map sheet 55,
ref. NS 906919*
*Admission. No facilities for entry whilst work is in progress. May be
closely viewed from the outside.*

Cl.2.   Dollar, CASTLE CAMPBELL   *(P.S.A.)*
The 15th century tower is in a good state of preservation and contains a
fine stone vaulted ceiling; other parts are 16th and 17th century.
*Situation. 1 mile north of Dollar, on the steep northern slope of the Ochil
Hills at the head of Dollar Glen. O.S. 1" map sheet 55, ref. NS 961993.*
Admission. Standard. 10p. Official Guide Book 9p.

Dollar, GLEN   *(N.T.S.)*
This is one of four delightful Lowland glens in the Ochils (Tillicoultry, Alva and
Menstrie are the others). A circuit of paths and bridges maintained by the
National Trust for Scotland leads to Castle Campbell at the head of the glen.

Cl.3.   Menstrie, MENSTRIE CASTLE
The Castle is not a National Trust for Scotland property but the Trust in
co-operation with Clackmannanshire County Council played a large part in
saving it from demolition. The Trust devised and furnished Commemoration
Rooms, opened in 1963, recalling that it was the birthplace of Sir William
Alexander who became James VI's Lieutenant for the Plantation of Nova
Scotia. This project was furthered by the creation of the Nova Scotian
Baronetcies and the coats-of-arms of 107 existing baronets are displayed.
*Situation. In Menstrie village (off A91). O.S. 1" map sheet 54, ref. NS 849968.
Commemoration rooms open May-Sept., Wed., Sat. and Sun. 2.30-5.
(Also on application to caretaker in flat in Castle).*

DUMFRIESSHIRE

Maps 2, 4 & 5

Dum.1. CAERLAVEROCK NATURE RESERVE

(N.C.C.)

Caerlaverock comprises Merse (saltmarsh) and extensive sandy foreshore between the River Nith and the Lochar Water. The sequence of vegetational types from seaward to landward illustrates the way in which the marsh has developed. The bird life is no less interesting; the area is a noted winter haunt for wildfowl, particularly barnacle geese. Access is unrestricted except to the sanctuary area. A limited number of permits to shoot wildfowl on a central section of the Reserve may be obtained on application to the Secretary, The Caerlaverock Panel, The Nature Conservancy Council, 12 Hope Terrace, Edinburgh EH9 2AS.

Pamphlet 3p from N.C.C., Edinburgh and Warden.

CAERLAVEROCK WILDFOWL REFUGE

(Wildfowl Trust)

The refuge at Eastpark Farm includes 600 acres of tidal Merse (the Sanctuary area of the National Nature Reserve) plus 235 acres of adjoining farmland. Large numbers of barnacle geese and pinkfooted geese visit the area as well as whooper and Bewick swans, and there is a small collection of British wildfowl. The Trust have developed a system of hides and observation points with access between earth screen banks to prevent disturbance to the geese.

Situation. 8 miles south east of Dumfries; turn off B275 at "Eastpark" signpost. O.S. 1" map sheet 75, ref. NY 052656.
Admission. At 11 am and 2 pm only from 1 September to 15 May. Closed on Tuesday and Wednesday of each week. Parties over 5 in number are advised to book in advance. Prior booking with the Refuge Manager, Mr Colin Campbell (Tel. Glencaple 200) is advisable. N.B. The Refuge is closed from 16 May to 31 August and parties of more than 50 cannot be accepted. Adults 45p, children 22½p. Wildfowl Trust Members admitted free.

Caerlaverock, CASTLE

(P.S.A.)

One of the foremost examples of medieval secular architecture in Scotland. The shape of the castle is very remarkable, being triangular, like a shield.

Situation. 7 miles south-south-east of Dumfries, on the Glencaple road. O.S. 1" map sheet 75, ref. NY 026656.
Admission. Standard. Bus service from Dumfries to Glencaple; thence three miles' walk. 10p. Official Guide Book 14p.

Dum.2. Canonbie, KNOTTY HOLM PICNIC SITE

(Dumfries C.C.)

A picnic area beside the A7 trunk road about ½ mile north of Canonbie.

Dum.3. Dumfries, AE FOREST WALKS

(F.C.)

Large new forest surrounded by open grazing. Spruce woods, roe and fallow deer, fox, hare, weasel: woodpigeon, jay, yellowhammer, sparrow-hawk, pheasant, partridge. Waymarked forest walks start from the picnic site on the bank of the water of Ae.

Situation. Forest Office, Ae Village, 2½ miles off A701 Dumfries-Moffat Road at Ae Bridgend.

Dum.4.   Dumfries, FOUNTAINBLEAU & LADYPARK RESERVE   *(S.W.T.)*

Accessible from a track by the north side of Dumfries High School on the
east of Dumfries.
Marshy woodland, on the outskirts of Dumfries, with varied botanical and
ornithological interest. Permit required. Obtainable from Dumfries Branch
Secretary, Mr J. Lyall, 6 Dalgarnock Place, Thornhill, Dumfriesshire.
Pamphlet 2½p from Branch Secretary. Gumboots necessary.

Dumfries, LINCLUDEN COLLEGE   *(P.S.A.)*

This 15th century collegiate church and provost's house are remarkable for
their heraldic adornment, and for the tomb of Princess Margaret, daughter
of Robert III.
*Situation. 1 mile north-north-west of central Dumfries. O.S. 1" map sheet 74,
ref. NX 997779.*
Admission. Standard. 5p. Leaflet. 1p.

Dum.5.   Ecclefechan, CARLYLE'S BIRTHPLACE   *(N.T.S.)*

Thomas Carlyle was born in the Arched House on December 4, 1795. The house
was built by his father and uncle, who were both master masons, and now
contains a collection of his belongings and manuscript letters.
*Situation. In Ecclefechan village; 19 miles North of Carlisle on A74.
O.S. 1" map sheet 75, ref. NY 195744.*
*Admission. Open March-October daily, except Sundays, 10-6. Other times by
appointment. Admission 10p. Children accompanied by adults, free.*

Dum.6.   Eaglesfield, KIRKCONNEL CHURCHYARD   *(P.S.A.)*

The present ruined chapel and churchyard are post-Reformation, but probably
stand on the site of an earlier foundation.
*Situation. Near Waterbeck, 1¾ miles north-east of Kirtlebridge.
O.S. 1" map sheet 75, ref. NY 250753.*
Admission. At all times without charge.

Dum.7.   Kirtlebridge, MERKLAND CROSS   *(P.S.A.)*

A fine 15th century floriated wayside cross, concerning which various legends
are current locally.
*Situation. In Annandale, north of the A74, 2 miles north-west of
Kirkpatrick-Fleming. O.S. 1" map sheet 75, ref NY 250721.*
Admission. All times without charge.

Dum.8.   Langholm, PENTON LYNNS PICNIC SITE   *(Dumfries C.C.)*

Picnic area and woodland walk by the Liddel Water.
Car park beside B6318, OS 1" map sheet 76, ref. NY 433775.

Dum.9.   Lochmaben, CASTLE & HIGHTAE LOCHS NATURE RESERVE   *(Dumfries C.C.)*

The Reserve consists of two separate lochs, Castle Loch and Hightae Loch,
with narrow marginal belts of marsh and wood. These are excellent examples
or rich (eutrophic) lowland lochs and their associated plants and animals.
The wintering wildfowl and breeding birds are of particular interest.

Dum.10. Moffat, GREY MARE'S TAIL (N.T.S.)

A dramatic 200-foot waterfall formed by the Tail burn dropping from Loch Skeen to meet Moffat water, seen on the road between St Mary's Loch and Moffat. An area of more than 2,300 acres around the falls was purchased in 1962 by the National Trust for Scotland to ensure continued public access. One of the few herds of wild goats in Scotland frequents the surrounding hills, and a wide variety of wild flowers is to be found around the falls. Access at all times. Care is required on path to Loch Skene.

Ranger-Naturalist Service during summer.

Dum.11. Mouswald, RUTHWELL CROSS (P.S.A.)

The Cross dates probably from the end of the 7th century and is one of the major monuments of Dark Age Europe.

Situation. In Ruthwell Church, ½ mile north of the village and 9 miles south-east of Dumfries. O.S. 1" map sheet 75, ref. NY 101682.
Admission. All times without charge. Key of Church must be obtained from the key-keeper, Kirkyett Cottage, Ruthwell. Leaflet.

DUNBARTONSHIRE Maps 4, 5 & 8

Du.1. Balloch, AUCHENDENNAN (DUCK BAY) PICNIC SITE
(Vale of Leven D.C.)
Picnic place beside Loch Lomond on the A82 road about 2 miles north-west of Balloch.

Balloch, DRUMKINNON PICNIC SITE *(Vale of Leven D.C.)*
Picnic place near the "Maid of the Loch" pier, ½ mile north of Balloch.

Balloch, LOCH LOMOND PARK *(Glasgow Corporation)*
Balloch Nature Trail is within easy access of Glasgow and is designed to let school children make discoveries for themselves and, by using keys in the guide, to identify animals and plants they find. There are slipways and a picnic site.
Booklet 7p from Glasgow Corporation Parks Department or trail information hut, Balloch. Superintendent's House. Tel. 041-258 2977.

Du.2. Cumbernauld, PALACERIGG COUNTRY PARK
(Burgh of Cumbernauld)
This Country Park is expected to open in early summer 1974. Extensive tree planting has already been carried out and nature trails and picnic sites have been prepared. A special feature of the Park is the comprehensive display of native wild and domestic animals. A ranger service operates in the Park.

Du.3. Garelochhead, WHISTLEFIELD PICNIC SITE/VIEWPOINT
(Helensburgh D.C.)
Picnic area beside the A814 road, ½ mile north of Garelochhead.

Du.4. Helensburgh, ARDMORE NATURE RESERVE *(S.W.T.)*
Fresh and saltwater marsh and foreshore of biological and geological interest. Free access to foreshore. Permit required for remainder of reserve (obtainable from Clyde Area Branch Secretary, John M. Findlay, 1 Westbank Quadrant, Glasgow, W.2.) except on open days, when the public will be particularly welcomed, the dates of which will be notified in the local press.
A booklet describing the reserve and its wildlife along the route of the nature trail is available from the above address, price 15p plus postage.

Du.5. LOCH LOMOND NATURE RESERVE *(N.C.C.)*
This Reserve at the south-east corner of Loch Lomond, near Balmaha, consists of five islands in Stirlingshire and Dunbartonshire: Inchcailloch, Torrinch, Creinch, Clairinsh and the Aber Isle, with part of the mainland shore and marshy hinterland on the south side of the Endrick water. The larger islands bear fine examples of semi-natural deciduous woodlands with oak dominant. There are 37 different kinds of trees and nearly 300 different ferns and flowering plants have been recorded. The islands lie along the Highland Boundary Fault, one of the two major structural features of Scotland. The slow flowing river and lagoons of the mainland are especially rich in aquatic life and the area is famed for wintering wildfowl and passage migrants. The nature trail on Inchcailloch deals with the geology of the island and describes the animals, plants and relics of human habitation. Day visitors who treat the island with respect are welcome but prior permission must be obtained for visits to the mainland area.

Booklets. "Loch Lomond National Nature Reserve" 4p; "Inchcailloch Nature Trail" 3p (N.C.C.), A. J. MacFarlane, The Boatyard, Balmaha. Tel. Balmaha 214. Reserve leaflet only, Balmaha Filling Station, and Mrs Braithwaite, The Pottery, Drymen. Trail leaflet only (in summer), Pier, North Bay, Inchcailloch. Warden, Mr. J. Mitchell, 22 Muirpark Way, Drymen.Tel. 036 06 425.

EAST LOTHIAN

Maps 5 & 6

EL.1. ABERLADY BAY NATURE RESERVE (E. Lothian C.C.)

Although much of the Reserve is intertidal estuary of mud, rock and sand, it also includes a small area of salt marsh, dune and fresh water hydrosere. The bay is especially notable as a wintering place for waders and wildfowl; the botanical and geological interest is also considerable.

EL.2. Cockburnspath, BILSDEAN PICNIC SITE (E. Lothian C.C.)

Picnic area adjacent to the A1 trunk road about 1½ miles north of Cockburnspath.

Cockburnspath, DUNGLASS COLLEGIATE CHURCH (P.S.A.)

Founded in 1450 it consists of nave, choir, transepts, sacristy and a central tower. The interior embellishments are very rich.

Situation. In the Dunglass estate 1 mile north-west of Cockburnspath, on the A1 between Dunbar and Berwick-upon-Tweed. O.S. 1" map sheet 63, ref. NT 767719.
Admission. All times without charge. Leaflet.

EL.3. Cockenzie, SETON COLLEGIATE CHURCH (P.S.A.)

The Church dates from the late 14th century and is one of the most important ecclesiastical monuments in the near vicinity of Edinburgh.

Situation. 1 mile south-east of Cockenzie, on the main Edinburgh-North Berwick road by St Germain's level crossing. O.S. 1" map sheet 62, ref. NT 418751.
Admission. Standard 5p. Leaflet. 1p.

Cockenzie, LONGNIDDRY SEASHORE AND BENTS (E. Lothian C.C.)

The area commands a fine view of the Forth and is frequented by numerous bird species. There are three car parks, for which there is a nominal charge.
Leaflet 1p from County Planning Office, Haddington.

EL.4. Dirleton, CASTLE (P.S.A.)

One of the most beautiful ruins in Scotland. The castle had an eventful history from its first siege by Edward I in 1298 until its destruction in 1650.

Situation. In the village of Dirleton, on the Edinburgh-North Berwick road. O.S. 1" map sheet 63, ref. NT 516839.
Admission. Standard. 10p. Official Guide Book 9p.

Dirleton, YELLOWCRAIG NATURE TRAIL (E. Lothian C.C.)

A coastal area, mature and newly established woodlands, dunes, links, seashore and outcrops of rock; part of the core of a volcano which erupted some 340 million years ago. Describing a varied coastal habitat with woodland, the trail booklet also covers the geology and geography of the area, and takes the opportunity to explain the principles of dune restoration.

Booklet 10p (East Lothian County Council and SWT) from Yellowcraig Car Park and County Buildings.

42

EL.5. Dunbar, WHITE SANDS AND BARNS NESS   *(E. Lothian C.C.)*
A limestone coastal area of special geological interest with interesting
fossils, birds, plant communities and a restored limekiln.
Barns Ness geological trail is included in a booklet which also identifies the
wildlife in the area. A nearby lime kiln has been reconstructed and is featured
in the booklet.
Booklet 10p (E.L.C.C. and S.W.T.) from camp site and Ranger, Barns Ness.

EL.6. East Linton, HAILES CASTLE   *(P.S.A.)*
This fortified manor-house is of exceptional interest because its oldest portions
date from before the War of Independence.
*Situation. 1½ miles south-west of East Linton. O.S. 1" map sheet 63,
ref. NT 575758.
Admission. Standard. 5p. Official Guide Pamphlet 1p.*

East Linton, PENCRAIG PICNIC SITE   *(E. Lothian C.C.)*
The first picnic site to be laid out by East Lothian County Council as part of their
tourist development proposals. Facilities include a viewpoint with explanatory
boards, picnic tables and walks through the woods.
Leaflet 2p from County Planning Office, Haddington.

East Linton, PRESSMENNAN WOOD NATURE TRAIL   *(F.C.)*
This two mile scenic trail leads through mixed woodland which contains an
artificial lake. The guide describes the trees, plants and animals and identifies
the landmarks seen from the viewpoint.
*Situation. 1 mile from Stenton village which lies on B6370 Dunbar-Gifford
road. 6 miles from Dunbar.
Leaflet 5p from F.C. District Office, Glentress, Peebles or honesty box at start
of trail.*

East Linton, PRESTON MILL   *(N.T.S.)*
A picturesque water-mill, possibly the only one of its kind still in working
condition in Scotland.
*Admission 15p, children 5p. Open 10-12.30, 2-7.30, Sundays 2-7.30.
(Except October-March when it closes at 4.30). Warden: Mr. T. Hunter.*
Nearby is Phantassie Doocot, an excellent example of a traditional Scottish
dovecot.

EL.7. Haddington, THE CHESTERS   *(P.S.A.)*
One of the best examples in Scotland of an Iron Age Fort, with multiple
ramparts, and clear remains of a considerable number of buildings in the
interior.
*Situation. 1 mile south of Drem. O.S. 1" map sheet 63, ref. NT 507782.
Admission. All times without charge.*

Haddington, ST. MARTIN'S CHURCH   *(P.S.A.)*
The ruined nave of a Romanesque church, altered in the 13th century when
the structure was vaulted and buttresses added. The chancel has disappeared.
*Situation. On the eastern outskirts of Haddington. O.S. 1" map sheet 63,
ref. NT 521739.
Admission. All times without charge.*

EL.8. Innerwick, EAST LAMMERMUIR DEANS NATURE RESERVE
                                                                 (S.W.T.)
Four deep valleys, in the Lammermuir Hills, with a rich flora of lime-loving
species, especially mosses and liverworts. Permit required. Obtainable from
Branch Secretary, c/o S.W.T., 8 Dublin Street, Edinburgh, EH1 3PP.

EL.9.   North Berwick, TANTALLON CASTLE   (P.S.A.)

This famous stronghold of the Douglases dates from the 14th century, and is one of the grandest things of its kind in Scotland.
Situation. On the coast, about 3 miles east of North Berwick. O.S. 1" map sheet 63, ref. NT 596850.
Admission. Standard. 10p. Official Guide 9p.

EL.10.   Pencaitland, PENCAITLAND-ORMISTON RAILWAY WALK
(E. Lothian C.C.)

This 5½ mile stretch of disused single-track railway, which was the first to be purchased for recreational purposes in Scotland, runs through a varied agricultural and afforested landscape. Information boards describe the history of the nearby mines and the wildlife of the area. Walking, cycling and horse-riding are allowed.

Pencaitland, WOODHALL PICNIC SITE   *(E. Lothian C.C.)*

Reclamation of this former colliery site has produced an attractive picnic area. There is a tree house for children to play in and access to the Pencaitland-Ormiston Railway Walk.
Leaflet 2p from County Planning Office, Haddington.

EL.11.   Prestonpans, PRESTONGRANGE BEAM ENGINE   *(E. Lothian C.C.)*

This colliery Beam Pumping Engine, manufactured in 1874 and in operation until 1954, has been scheduled as an Industrial Monument and it and its engine house are being restored, partly by voluntary labour. Working models, photographs and other items are being collected to tell the story of coal-mining in E. Lothian, where the earliest recorded mining in Britain took place.
Situation. On B1348, 1 mile west of Prestonpans.
Information leaflet from County Planning Officer, Haddington, or David Spence, 24 Woodlands Grove, Edinburgh 15 (031-661 2718) who will arrange to show interested parties round.

EL.12.   Tranent, ORMISTON MARKET CROSS   (P.S.A.)

A fine free-standing 15th century cross, with a blank shield of arms, now erected on a modern base in the main street of village.
Situation. In the village of Ormiston, about 2 miles south of Tranent. O.S. 1" map sheet 62, ref. NT 414693.
Admission. All times without charge.

ISLANDS

EL.13.   BASS ROCK   *(Major Sir Hew Hamilton Dalrymple, Bart.)*

The Bass is one of the landmarks of the Forth. About 350 feet high and a mile round, it is a great gannetry. In 1671 it was sold by the Provost of Edinburgh to the Government and became a State prison for Covenanters. In 1691 a group of Jacobite prisoners seized it and held it for three years, plundering passing shipping for supplies.

EL.14.   FIDRA, EYEBROUGHTY AND LAMB ISLANDS   (R.S.P.B.)

Eiders nest, and normally four species of tern. Boat sails past Lamb Island (no landing allowed) where three species of auks nest, as well as kittiwakes, shags, and cormorants. Off Eyebroughty, thousands of eider gather in autumn to moult. (Seen from the shore, one mile west of Yellowcraig.)

FIFE   Maps 4, 5 & 6

Fi.1. Aberdour, CASTLE *(P.S.A.)*

The oldest part is a rhomboidal tower of the 14th century, to which other
buildings have been added in the 16th and 17th centuries.
*Situation. In the village of Aberdour, on the Firth of Forth, between
Inverkeithing and Burntisland. O.S. 1" map sheet 55, ref. NT 193854.
Admission. Standard. 5p. Official Guide Book 11p.*

Aberdour, ST BRIDGET'S CHURCH *(P.S.A.)*

This ancient church (the eastern part of the existing monument) was
dedicated to St Bridget in 1244.
*Situation. On the shores of the Forth, 2 miles south-west of Aberdour.
O.S. 1" map sheet 62, ref. NT 169838.
Admission. All times without charge.*

Fi.2. Anstruther, THE SCOTTISH FISHERIES MUSEUM

(Scottish Fisheries Museum Trust Ltd.)

In St Ayles Land, one of the oldest identified property sites in any Scottish
burgh (with a charter dated 1318), there is now a collection of items
illustrating various aspects of the Scottish fisherman's life, both at home and
at sea, historical and modern, with whaling exhibits, model and full-size
fishing boats, ship's gear of all kinds, a marine aquarium and a fisheries
reference library.
*Situation. St Ayles, Harbourhead, Anstruther, Fife. Tel. Anstruther 310628.
Admission. May-September, 10-12.30, 2-6 weekdays, 2-5 Sundays.
October-April 2.30-4.30 everyday except Tuesdays, Christmas Day and New
Years' Day. (Visits outside these times by prior arrangement.) 17p, children
and OAPs 10p. Members of the Museum Trust and National Trust for
Scotland free.*

Fi.3. Ceres, BANKHEAD MOSS NATURE RESERVE *(S.W.T.)*

Raised bog, near Peat Inn, of interest for peat-bog flora, lichens and mosses.
Permits required. Obtainable from the Fife Branch Secretary, Mr J. Caldwell,
67 Milton Road, Kirkcaldy.
Situation. On west sde of Pitscottie-Peat Inn road, near Bankhead Farm.

Ceres, CRAIGHALL DEN NATURE TRAIL *(Cupar District Council/SWT)*

Nature trail in sheltered wooded den with botanical and geological interest,
and including a fine early-nineteenth century lime kiln. Trail open all year.
*Access from Ceres-Largo road. ½ mile south of Ceres village.
Booklet 8p available from the Post Office or Fife Folk Museum, Ceres.*

Ceres, FIFE FOLK MUSEUM *(Central and North Fife Preservation Society)*

Several old buildings in Ceres, including part of the 17th century tolbooth, have
been reconstructed to house exhibits collected mainly from Central and
North Fife, illustrating many aspects of life in the county. Transport and
trade, industry and crafts, and domestic life are among the subjects dealt with
indoors, and a gallery outside contains agricultural implements.
*Situation. The Weigh House, Ceres. Admission, April-October (except
Tuesdays), Sundays 3-6, otherwise 2-5. 10p. Members, students and
children 5p.*

Fi.4. Cupar, SCOTSTARVIT TOWER *(P.S.A.)*

This fine tower is known to have been in existence in 1579.
Situation. 2 miles south of Cupar, off the Cupar-Kennoway road.
O.S. 1" map sheet 56, ref. NO 370113.
Admission. All reasonable times without charge on application to
custodian. Leaflet.

Fi.5. Culross, ROYAL BURGH *(N.T.S.)*

This small Royal Burgh on the north shore of the Forth is the most striking
and complete introduction one could wish to find to the ways of Scottish
domestic life in the 16th and 17th centuries. The overall layout of the town
has changed hardly at all in 300 years. Salt-panning and coal-mining were
the industrial basis of its prosperity in the 16th century. Developed under
the business-like laird Sir George Bruce, the salt and coal of Culross
nurtured a flourishing sea-going trade with other Forth ports and also
over the North Sea to Scandinavia, Germany and the Netherlands. The
ARK and the NUNNERY have been rescued from almost irrevocable
dereliction to renew and secure the character of the Cross as the heart of the
old burgh. Opposite stands the STUDY with its comely tower, associated
with Bishop Leighton and now the home of the Trust's resident representative.
Here the visitor will see a display of furniture, maps, pottery and pewter
illustrating early life in Culross; and guidance will be given on a tour
round the town.
The Culross room and Outlook room in the Study are open March-October,
weekdays 10-12.30, 2-7; Sundays 2-7; November-February, Saturdays
10-12.30, 2-4; Sundays 2-4. Also by arrangement. Donation Box.
"Guide to Culross" 15p (N.T.S.) and "Culross Walkabout" 10p (N.T.S.).

Culross, THE ABBEY *(P.S.A.)*

The Cistercian monastery was founded by Malcolm, Earl of Fife, in 1217.
There remains of it the choir, still used as the parish church, and parts,
more or less, of the nave, the cellarium, the frater and the dorter. Only the
south wall of the nave belongs to the early 13th century; the rest of the
buildings date mostly from about 1300, and were reconstructed in the reign
of James IV.
Admission. Standard. Leaflet 1p.
Applications to visit the parish church should be made at the Manse.

Culross, ST MUNGO'S CHAPEL *(N.T.S.)*

On the outskirts of the town, the now ruined chapel was built by
Robert Blackadder, the first Archbishop of Glasgow, in 1503, to honour
St Mungo, who was born in Culross and who founded Glasgow Cathedral.

Culross, THE PALACE *(P.S.A.)*

This charming mansion was built between 1597 and 1611 by George Bruce
of Culross and its painted ceilings are as fine as anything of their kind
in Scotland.
Situation. In the village of Culross, on the Firth of Forth, between
Kincardine and Dunfermline. O.S. 1" map sheet 55, ref. NS 985859.
Admission. Standard. 10p. Leaflet.

Fi.6. Dunfermline, ABBEY *(P.S.A.)*

This great Benedictine house owes its foundations to Queen Margaret, and the
foundations of her church remain beneath the present late Norman nave.
Situation. In Dunfermline. O.S. 1" map sheet 55, ref. NT 090873.
Admission. To nave: standard, weekdays. Sundays, Summer 2-6.
Winter 2-4.30. Without charge. Leaflet 1p.

Fi.7. Falkland, LOMOND HILLS PICNIC SITE (Fife CC)

Opening in 1974. Small picnic area, beside the hill road from Falkland to Leslie, with extensive footpath network.

Falkland, PALACE (N.T.S.)

Falkland recalls vividly the turbulence and romance of the Royal Stuarts who built the palace as a hunting lodge in the 15th and 16th centuries. The South Range which survives almost intact, was begun by James IV and completed by his son James V who added the courtyard facade, "a display of early renaissance architecture without parallel in the British Isles". The palace garden includes the site of the "lang butts" where James V and his courtiers practised their archery and makes an attractive setting for the striking profile of the palace against a background of the Lomond Hills.

Admission. March-mid October 10-6, Sundays 2-6. Palace and gardens 40p, children 10p. Gardens 20p, children 5p. School parties: 5p. Car park 10p. Guidebook 20p. Principal guide, Mr Norman Lothian. Telephone: Falkland 397.

The East Port is the Trust's Information and Reception Centre. Falkland is as rich if not richer in Little Houses than is Culross or Dunkeld. St Andrew's House is typical of the dwellings occupied by the Royal Household, as is Moncreif House across the street. Brunton House reveals its Court associations in its former name of Falconer's House. In High Street are the two Weaver's Cottages, with red pantiled roofs, which provided the combined home and workshop of the handloom weaver, once common throughout Fife.

Fife Coastal Burghs, "LITTLE HOUSES"

An interesting architectural expedition along the Fife coast of the Forth can be based on the work of restoration, in hand and completed, covered by the National Trust for Scotland's "little houses improvement scheme". The first two properties to be re-habilitated under the scheme were in CRAIL, where two ruinous 17th century houses at Rumford were restored as two flats. In PITTENWEEM, 4-8 High Street were restored as two houses and the Giles tenement block as three flats and a house: this block, with Gyles House, now forms the most distinctive group in the whole of this area. Nos. 3-5 East Shore, a handsome early 19th century house has been renewed and remodelled internally. The most important restoration is Kellie Lodging in the High Street, a 16th century building of great architectural quality. In ANSTRUTHER the kenspeckle Buckie House, and its next door neighbour, have been restored and remodelled. Its shell decoration has been refurbished. Other properties in Anstruther, nearby CELLARDYKE, and ST MONANS were acquired and modernised internally and their external character preserved. At DYSART. the Anchorage has been restored. The Trust has also restored, for the Crown Estates Commissioners, the Customs House, Crail, and the row of fishermen's dwellings, known as the Pan Ha', which run along the shore of Dysart from St Serf's Tower eastwards. The four local Preservation Societies — for St Andrews, Crail, the East Neuk and Central and North Fife — are each doing valuable work in the same line. Efforts have been concentrated in East Fife, as its small coastal burghs contain a wealth of good, early building.

See also "What to see in East Fife" which describes twelve trails for motorists and walkers.

Leaflet 5p from East Fife Preservation Society and local information centres.

Fi.8.   Kingsbarns, BEACH PICNIC SITE   *(Fife CC)*

Opening in 1974. Picnic area near the shore with access to beach and to footpath from St Andrews to Crail.

Fi.9.   Kirkcaldy, DUNNIKIER PARK NATURE TRAIL
(Corporation of Kirkcaldy)

Laid out in the grounds of Dunnikier House, the trail identifies many of the plants and lists birds that are likely to be seen.

Booklet 5p (S.W.T. and Kirkcaldy Parks Committee) from Parks Department, Kirkcaldy and S.W.T.

Kirkcaldy, RAVENSCRAIG PARK NATURE TRAIL
(Corporation of Kirkcaldy)

Set in a Park with an unusual variety of exotic trees, the trail identifies many of them and features other points of interest.

Booklet 2½p from Parks Department, Kirkcaldy.

Fi.10.   Leuchars, FOREST WALKS

Two nature trails laid out by the Tayport Preservation and Development Society serve as an introduction to the plants and trees in the forest and give notes on the birds and animals found in nearby Morton Lochs Nature Reserve.

Leuchars, MORTON LOCHS NATURE RESERVE   *(N.C.C.)*

Artificial loch on migration route of wildfowl and waders.

Permit required to visit parts away from road. Apply Nature Conservancy Council, 12 Hope Terrace, Edinburgh EH9 2AS. Warden, Kinshaldy Cottage, Tentsmuir Forest, Leuchars, Fife.

Leuchars, TENTSMUIR FOREST   *(F.C.)*

Car park and picnic area (10p) giving access to forest and sea beaches.

*Situation. 4 miles east of A92; 7 miles south-east of Dundee.
Toilets (facilities for disabled).*

Leuchars, TENTSMUIR POINT NATURE RESERVE   *(N.C.C.)*

An outstanding area for the study of coastal sand movements and plant colonization. The Reserve comprises a large area of foreshore (the Abertay Sands) — which is a winter roost for wildfowl — a landward area of dunes with alder and willow slacks, and small patches of marsh. Wheeled transport on the sands within the Reserve and access to the Abertay Sands are prohibited.

Access. Byelaws prohibit landing on Abertay Sands. Danger of unexploded missiles on the southern part of the Reserve. Warden: Mr M. Smith, Kinshaldy Cottage, Tentsmuir Forest, Leuchars, Fife.

Fi.11.   Pittenweem, KELLIE CASTLE   *(N.T.S.)*

A very fine example of the domestic architecture of the Lowland Counties
of Scotland; the oldest part is believed to date from about 1360, and the
building is mainly of the 16th and 17th Century. Many of the internal
features, in particular the plaster work and panelling painted with
"romantic" landscapes, are excellent examples of their period. The walled
garden made by the late Sir Robert Lorimer, who restored and made his home
at Kellie Castle, is a delightful example of late Victoriana.
Situation. 3 miles NNW of Pittenweem.
Admission. Castle: April-September daily (except Monday and Tuesday) 2-6.
Gardens: 10-6. Castle and Garden 30p; children 10p. Garden 15p; children
accompanied by an adult, free. Guide book 20p.
Resident Custodian: Mr Hew Lorimer, R.S.A. Telephone: Arncroach 271.

ISLANDS

Fi.12.   Inchcolm, ABBEY   *(P.S.A.)*

The monastic buildings, which include a fine 13th century octagonal chapter
house, are the best preserved in Scotland.
Situation. On an island in the Firth of Forth, south of Aberdour.
O.S. 1" map sheet 62, ref. NT 190826.
Access. Local boat hirer operates from Aberdour during summer months.
Details of tides may be obtained from the Abbey custodian.
Admission. Standard. 5p. Official Guide Book 14p.

Fi.13.   ISLE OF MAY NATURE RESERVE   *(N.C.C.)*

This island first became a focus of ornithological attention about the end
of the last century and notable migration research has been carried out
here since 1907. In 1947 a Bird Observatory and Field Station was set up
under a Joint Committee which now manages the Reserve on behalf of the
Council. There is no Warden.
Access. Via boat from Crail. Small parties can be accommodated.
Prospectus from Regional Officer for East Scotland. The Nature Conservancy
Council, 12 Hope Terrace, Edinburgh EH9 2AS and Mr A. MacDonald,
Bookings Secretary, 5 Larkfield Road, Eskbank, Dalkeith, Midlothian.

INVERNESS-SHIRE Maps 7, 8, 9, 11 & 12

MAINLAND

In.1. Aviemore, CRAIGELLACHIE NATURE RESERVE (N.C.C.)
This Reserve includes an expanse of birchwoods stretching along the steep eastern slopes of Craigellachie and Craeg nan Gabhar. Above the woods, moorlands reach an elevation of over 1,700 feet and include the northern part of Lochan Dubh. The whole area is of exceptional biological interest, particularly because of its insect fauna. The Craigellachie Birchwood Nature Trail, laid out near the Aviemore Centre, demonstrates the plant and animal communities associated with a Highland birchwood. A viewpoint on the trail affords a good panorama of the Cairngorms.
Booklet 3p from the Aviemore Centre.

In.2. Beauly, PRIORY (P.S.A.)
A house of the Valliscaulian Order founded in 1230. The plan represents the earliest form of Cistercian church in Britain.
Situation. In Beauly. O.S. 1" map sheet 27, ref. NH 528466.
Admission. Standard. 5p. Official Guide Pamphlet 2½p.

Beauly, REELIG GLEN FOREST TRAIL (F.C.)
A series of walks through a fertile wooded glen noteworthy for its stands of Douglas fir, and for its geological, botanical and archaeological interest.
Situation. 8 miles west of Inverness on Moniack-Clunes road off A9 (Inverness-Beauly). Leaflet 5p from local hotels and tourist offices.

In.3. CAIRNGORMS NATURE RESERVE (N.C.C.)
This is the largest National Nature Reserve in Great Britain and one of the largest in Europe. The vegetation includes the native Scots pine, juniper and birchwoods, moorland and the interesting Arctic-alpine plants of the corries, screes and exposed summits. The fauna is rich in variety of species, including wild cat, red and roe deer, reindeer, ptarmigan, dotterel, crested tit, Scottish crossbill and golden eagle. The Nature Trail at Achlean can provide a good opportunity (according to the season) for seeing red deer from the observation tower. At Loch an Eilein a trail helps to identify the more common plants and animals found in this Highland setting of loch and island, and the Visitor Centre exhibit tells the story of the native pinewoods.
Visitor Centre open 10.30-1 and 2-6, Wed. to Sat. only in May; daily June-Sept. inclusive.
Access to parts of the Reserve in Mar and Glenfeshie is restricted in August, September and October. During late summer and autumn visitors should contact the Chief Warden at Kinakyle, Aviemore (Tel. 250) or the Warden, Mr D. Rose, Lilybank, Braemar. Leaflet "Cairngorm National Nature Reserve" 10p, trail booklets 3p.

In.4. Carrbridge, LANDMARK (Visitor Centres Ltd.)
In Europe's first visitor centre, the exhibition and slide-programme are designed to make the visitor aware of the story of Strathspey from glacial times to the present day; this story is continued outside on the board-walk nature trail through the pine wood. A well-stocked bookshop allows the visitor to follow up his interest in Scottish history, natural history and conservation. Programmes of nature films are shown. Interested school parties should make arrangements in advance with the manager. The centre also includes a restaurant and gift shop.
Situation. On A9, on Southern outskirts of Carrbridge.
Admission. Exhibition and slide-programme: adults 25p, children 12½p.
Car park 10p, open all year.

In.5.   Culloden, BATTLEFIELD   (N.T.S.)

The field of Culloden, where Prince Charles Edward's cause was finally
crushed, is held and maintained as a national historic site by the National
Trust for Scotland. Among the principal features of interest are the Graves
of the Clans — communal burial places with simple headstones bearing
individual clan names — alongside the main road. It was on 16th April, 1746
only eight months after his Standard was raised at Glenfinnan, that
Prince Charles and his Highland army were defeated here by the forces of
George II, under Cumberland. The battle lasted only forty minutes. In that
time, and in the pursuit that followed, it has been estimated that the
Highlanders lost some 1,200 men, and the King's army suffered 310 casualties.
A few days after the battle the survivors of the Prince's army were disbanded
at Ruthven on Speyside to bring an end to his active contest for the throne.
*Admission. Visitor Centre open March 31 to May 31, 9.30-6.30, June to
September 30, 9.30-9.30; October 1-19, 9.30-6.30 (Sundays 2-6.30).
Admission. Visitor Centre and Old Leanach Museum (includes audio-visual
exhibition in centre) 20p, parties of 20 or more paying as a group, 10p per
head, children 5p. Sundays (no illustrated exhibition) 10p, parties 5p,
children free. Car park 10p. Old Leanach museum only: adults 10p, children
5p (visitors calling at museum first should present museum tickets at visitor
centre). Battlefield, memorial cairn and clan graves. Site open all year.
Guide book 15p, coloured map folder 5p. Warden: Mr. D. Stewart.*

Culloden, CLAVA CAIRNS   (P.S.A.)

A group of burial cairns in which three concentric rings of great stones are now
the principal features exposed; late Neolithic or Early Bronze Age.
*Situation. 5½ miles east of Inverness, on the south bank of the River Nairn,
opposite Culloden battlefield. O.S. 1" map sheet 28, ref. NH 756445.
Admission. All times without charge. Leaflet.*

Culloden, FOREST TRAIL   (F.C.)

Trees along this two mile trail have been named to assist in identification.
The route includes sites associated with Prince Charles and the Jacobite uprising.
*Situation. 3 miles east of Inverness on by-road off A96.
Leaflet 5p from Forest Office and locally.*

In.6.   Drumnadrochit, CORRIMONY CAIRN   (P.S.A.)

Megalithic chambered cairn, probably Neolithic, surrounded by a peristalith
of stone slabs, outside which is a circle of eleven standing stones.
*Situation. Glen Urquhart, 8 miles west of Drumnadrochit. O.S. 1" map sheet
27, ref. NH 383303.
Admission. All times without charge.*

In.7.   Drumnadrochit, URQUHART CASTLE   (P.S.A.)

One of the largest castles in Scotland, it played a great part in Scottish
history from the invasion of Edward I until the Jacobite rising of 1689.
*Situation. On the west shore of Loch Ness, 1½ miles south-east of
Drumnadrochit. O.S. 1" map sheet 27, ref. NH 531286.
Admission. Standard. 5p. Official Guide 14p.*

In.8.   Fort Augustus, INCHNACARDOCH FOREST TRAIL   (F.C.)

Two forest trails set in Scotland's first State Forest. A leaflet describes some of the
work of the Forestry Commission and explains points of interest along the
route.
*Situation. Off A82 just north of Fort Augustus. Leaflet 5p from Forest Office
and locally.*

In.9.   Fort William, INVERLOCHY CASTLE   (P.S.A.)
A well preserved example of a 13th century castle with a quadrangular wall
and round angle towers displaying characteristic longbow-slits.
*Situation. 1½ miles north-east of Fort William and 1½ miles south-west of
modern castle. O.S. 1" map sheet 35, ref. NN 121755.*
Admission. Not yet open to the public. May be viewed from outside.

Fort William, GLEN ROY NATURE RESERVE   (N.C.C.)
A unique British example of post-glacial lake terraces, often called the
"parallel roads" and the subject of many legendary explanations. Car Park
(access by rough road), panoramic viewpoint with information plaque.

In.10.   Foyers, FARIGAIG FOREST CENTRE AND TRAIL   (F.C.)
The forest trail starts from the car park at the forest information centre and
leads through attractive mixed woodland of mature conifers and native
broadleaved trees. Mountain viewpoints overlook Loch Ness and the deep
gorges of the Farigaig and Allt Mor rivers.
Situation. On B852 2½ miles north of Foyers. Leaflet 5p.

In.11.   Glenelg, BROCHS: DUN TELVE AND DUN TRODDAN   (P.S.A.)
Two Iron Age broch towers, ruinous but with wall portions still standing
over 30 feet in height, and structural features well preserved.
*Situation. On the west coast of Inverness-shire, about 1½ miles south-east
of Glenelg which is 8 miles west of Shiel Bridge. O.S. 1" map sheet 35,
ref. NG 829172 and 834172.*
Admission. All times without charge.

In.12.   Glenfinnan, MONUMENT AND VISITOR CENTRE   (N.T.S.)
The Monument commemorates the raising of Prince Charles Edward's
standard at Glenfinnan on 19th August, 1745, as a rallying point for the clans
who followed him in the '45 Rising. The new Information Centre provides
an exposition of the Prince's campaign from Glenfinnan to Derby and back
to the final defeat at Culloden.
*Admission. 11 April-end May, 9.30-6; June-August, 9.30-8; September-
19 October, 9.30-6. Adults, 10p, (includes parking) children, 5p. Guide book
10p, map/folder 5p. Warden: Mr R. MacKellaig. Tel. Kinlocheil 250.*

In.13.   GLEN MORE FOREST PARK   (F.C.)
The Glen More Forest Park which lies to the east of the Spey valley in
Inverness-shire contains 3000 acres of woodland and 9000 acres of high ground.
At its heart lies Loch Morlich, fringed by remnants of the old Caledonian
pine forests, and round its perimeter the high rounded tops of the Cairngorms
rise to over 4000 feet. At the head of the loch there is a large caravan site,
a modern hostel for group accommodation, a Youth Hostel, a Scottish Sports
Council training centre, shop, tea room and information room. The loch
contains trout and pike and both boat and bank fishing are available; there is
good bathing from a sandy beach and safe sailing and canoeing. Three forest
trails and five longer treks lead from the caravan site, the former self guided
by booklet and the latter by colour coded marker posts. The park has an
extensive fauna and it is not unusual to see red and roe deer, reindeer, blue
hare, grouse, ptarmigan, capercaillie, golden eagle and occasionally a visiting
osprey. Beyond the forest a new road climbs to Coire Cas on Cairngorm where
there are extensive ski facilities.
*Situation. Glen More Caravan Site, Forest Information Centre, Norwegian
Hostel, start of forest trails and treks — on A951 ski road from Aviemore-
Cairngorm.*
*Publications. Glen More Forest Park Guide (42½p); Glen More Forest Park
Map (10p); Glen More Forest Park Trail Guide (5p).*

In.14.   Invergarry, GLENGARRY FOREST WALKS   *(F.C.)*
Starting from a small car park and picnic area in the Garry gorge, the route passes
through varied and attractive conifer woodland, dividing to pass above and
below a major waterfall. There are good views of Ben Tee and the forest.
*Situation. Off A82 at its junction with A87 north-west of Loch Oich. O.S. 1"
map sheet 36, ref. NH 307012.*

In.15.   Inverness, CRAIG PHADRIG FOREST TRAIL   *(F.C.)*
Overlooking Inverness, the forest trail leads to a vitrified Pictish Fort dating
from the Iron Age, and continues past forestry research plots.
Leaflet 5p from Tourist Offices.

In.16.   Inverness, FORT GEORGE   *(P.S.A.)*
Fort George was begun in 1748 as a result of the Jacobite rebellion. It is one
of the finest late artillery fortifications in Europe.
*Situation. 8½ miles north-east of Inverness, 6½ miles west of Nairn.
O.S. 1" map sheet 28, ref. NH 762567.
Admission. Standard. 10p. Official Guide 25p.*

In.17.   Inverness, KNOCKNAGAEL BOAR STONE   *(P.S.A.)*
A roughly shaped slab. At the top is incised the mirror-case symbol and
below the figure of a boar.
*Situation. On Knocknagael farm, beside a secondary road, about
2½ miles south-south-west of Inverness railway station.
O.S. 1" map sheet 28, ref. NH 657413.
Admission. All times without charge.*

In.18.   Kincraig, HIGHLAND WILDLIFE PARK
This 260 acre park contains a collection of Scotland's native wildlife, past and
present. After a long absence, lynx, bear, wolf and reindeer again share their
former habitat with fox, badger, eagle, wildcat and red deer.
*Situation. On the A9, almost mid-way between Aviemore and Kingussie.
Admission. Open daily March-October, 10-6 or 1½ hours before dusk, if
earlier. Cars £1.10, no limit to number of passengers. Mini-buses £1.10, up
to 6 passengers, extra passengers 30p each. Coaches, adults 30p, children
under 14 20p. Special prices for pre-booked parties (for details write to
Park Director).* **NB Visitors must be in closed vehicles.**

In.19.   Kingussie, AM FASGADH   *(Scottish Universities)*
The Gaelic means "The Shelter". This Highland Folk Museum contains a
comprehensive collection of objects in every-day use in the Highlands in
former times; Highland dress, tartans, relics of old crafts, farm implements, etc.
Period furnished cottage, a mill from Lewis, etc.; "black house", clack mill.
Admission. Open May-September, weekdays 10-4.

Kingussie, RUTHVEN BARRACKS   *(P.S.A.)*
Ruthven Barracks, built in 1719, were captured and burnt by Prince Charles
Edward in 1746. They were never re-occupied.
*Situation. ¾ mile south-east of Kingussie, access from B970.
O.S. 1" map sheet 37, ref. NN 765997.
Admission. All times without charge.*

In.20.   LOCH GARTEN NATURE RESERVE   *(R.S.P.B.)*
Established in 1959 to safeguard a pair of ospreys which have continued to
nest each year in a tall pine in the centre of the Reserve. From a special
Observation Post, equipped with high-powered binoculars, visitors can watch

the ospreys at their eyrie. Crested tits, capercaillie, siskin and crossbill are
frequently seen in the area.
*Access. Restricted, except by sign-posted track to Observation Post when
ospreys are in residence. Entry 10-8.30 (subject to variation) between
1st April and 31st August. Access by any other route is strictly forbidden.*

ISLANDS

In.21. Harris, ST CLEMENT'S CHURCH (P.S.A.)

The only cruciform medieval church in the Outer Isles. The rich decoration
of the church has obviously been derived from the work at Iona.
*Situation. Rodel, at the south end of the Isle of Harris. O.S. 1″ map sheet
17, ref. NG 047832.*
*Admission. All reasonable times without charge on application to custodian.
Leaflet.*

In.22. MONACH ISLES NATURE RESERVE (N.C.C.)

This Reserve comprises Shillay, the main islands of Ceann Iar and Ceann Ear
(joined at low tide), the reef of Stockay and several isolated rocks; only
about 836 acres are above high tide level. These uninhabited islands
provide an outstanding example of shell sand habitat and all the essential
features of uncultivated *machair*. They are also wintering grounds for
barnacle and white-fronted geese and form a link in the chain of wildfowl
refuges and there is a small nursery of grey seals.
*Permission to visit the Reserve should be obtained from the Warden at Loch
Druidibeg, and the Factor, North Uist Estates, Lochmaddy, North Uist.
(Tel. Lochmaddy 329).*

In.23. RHUM NATURE RESERVE (N.C.C.)

The mountains along the south-west coast of Rhum rise at three points above
2,500 feet and are of exceptional geological interest owing to their volcanic
origin and their composition of rare, ultra basic rocks. Rhum is an outstanding
area for geological and botanical research and is used as a centre for the
study of red deer. Important experiments and investigations into the
restoration of vegetation after over-grazing and over-burning are also
being carried out by Council scientists. Two nature trails introduce the
visitor to the variety of plants and animals on Rhum, making the point that
nature is not static. The South Side Trail starts at the point of disembarkation,
while the Kinloch Glen Nature Trail skirts Loch Scresort and leads up the
glen as far as visitors are allowed to go. *(Leaflets 5p from the Warden.)*
Access is via MacBrayne's steamers from Mallaig and by regular excursions
arranged by Mallaig boat hirers during the summer. For day visits,
no permission is necessary. There is no accommodation on the island
for visiting parties and day visits only are allowed, except by permit
from the Nature Conservancy Council, 12 Hope Terrace, Edinburgh EH9 2AS.
There is a post office and shop, where postcards, confectionery and provisions
can be purchased. The whole island is closed to visitors for short periods from the
end of March and again at the beginning of June and at any time parts of the
island may be closed, e.g. for stalking.
*Chief Warden: Mr G. MacNaughton, Lyon Cottage, Kinloch, Isle of Rhum,
Inverness-shire. Tel. Rhum 25.*

In.24. Skye, PORTREE NATURE TRAIL

A riverside nature trail, established by Portree High School as a contribution
to the 1970 Highland Village Competition. The amenity of the area has been
improved by tree planting.
Leaflet available from Portree Tourist Office.

In.25. ST. KILDA *(N.C.C. & N.T.S.)*

This remote little archipelago lies 110 miles out in the Atlantic west of the Scottish mainland. The main island of Hirta maintained its population over the centuries until 1930 when lack of man power dictated its evacuation. Fowling among the great colonies of sea-birds, puffins for feathers and meat, young fulmars for their oil, and young gannets for meat, herding sheep, crofting and fishing constituted the staple employment on the Island. Traces of the old ways of life built around this primitive subsistence economy are still to be seen all over the island. In addition to Hirta the group includes Soay, the sheep isle; Boreray, the gannet's isle, with its neighbouring stacs; Stac an Armin and Stac Lee; Dun and the Stac of Levenish.

Because of the particular scientific interest of the group's natural history the islands have been leased by the Trust to the Nature Conservancy Council, who are carrying out a long-term programme of research on the indigenous Soay sheep, the nesting seabirds and the vegetation. N.T.S. working parties have already done a considerable amount of maintenance on the village street, dykes and cleitan and more concerted efforts are planned. Successive Service detachments on the island, associated with the South Uist rocket range, have co-operated with the Trust and Nature Conservancy Council over the preservation of natural features and wild-life.

Access restricted. "Life and Death of St Kilda" £1.05 (N.T.S.). Leaflet 3p (N.C.C.), 12 Hope Terrace, Edinburgh EH9 2AS.

In.26. North Uist, BALRANALD NATURE RESERVE *(R.S.P.B.)*

Wide variety of typical Hebridean habitats ranging from sweeping white sands backed with dunes, stretches of machair with an abundance of wild flowers, to a variety of lochs of different types. Reserve was established to safeguard the red-necked phalaropes and their breeding habitat. One of the most important wetland reserves on the Outer Hebrides.

Access. R.S.P.B. Summer Warden in residence at Hougharry from April to August. Visitors are asked to contact him on arrival.

In.27. South Uist, LOCH DRUIDIBEG NATURE RESERVE *(N.C.C.)*

This reserve is notable as the most important surviving breeding ground in Britain of the native greylag goose. In addition to conserving the breeding population in this area, the Nature Conservancy Council are carrying out detailed research on the breeding status of geese in South Uist. For this reason permission to visit the reserve should be obtained during the breeding season.

Enquiries to the Warden, 135 Stilligarry, South Uist. (Telephone Grogarry 202.)

KINCARDINESHIRE

Map 10

Ke.1. Banchory, CRATHES CASTLE

(N.T.S.)

Crathes is a striking and dramatic survival of 16th century baronial architecture – its great defensive tower capped decoratively with small turrets and dormer windows, and it has a formal garden of rare distinction and variety. The famous painted ceilings of Crathes originate from the end of the 16th century. At the top of the tower there is the Long Gallery, once used as the baron court when the laird had power to exercise the death penalty.

Nature trails through the wooded policies identify many of the introduced trees and describe some of the natural history interest.
Situation. 3 miles east of Banchory. O.S. 1" map sheet 40, ref. NJ 734969.
Admission. April and October, Wednesday 11-1, 2-6; Saturday and Sunday 2-6. May-September, Weekdays 11-1, 2-6; Sunday 2-6. Gardens daily from 9.30. Restaurant open May onwards at castle opening times.
Castle and gardens 45p, children 15p. School parties: 10p. Gardens 25p, children 5p, Castle 30p, children 10p. Nature trail booklet 10p. Car park 10p. Guide book 25p. Trust representative: Tel. Crathes 225.

Banchory, SHOOTING GREENS FOREST WALKS, BLACKHALL FOREST

(F.C.)

Attractive woodland walks start from car park and picnic area.
Situation. 4 miles west of Banchory, 1 mile north of B976. O.S. 1" map sheet 39, ref. NJ 634944.

FORESTS IN THE NORTH-EAST

(F.C.)

Many of the great forests of the North East, owned by the Forestry Commission, include some of the loveliest Scottish woodland with Scots pine, European larch and Norway spruce and many other species including the great and noble silver firs, Western red cedar and Western hemlock. Vegetation includes chickweed wintergreen and twin-flower. Forests include Drumtochty, Laurencekirk (A94); Fetteresso, Stonehaven (A92).
Booklet "Forests of North East Scotland" 25p (F.C.). Forestry Commission, 6 Queen's Gate, Aberdeen AB9 2NQ.

Ke.2. Mearns, DRUMTOCHTY FOREST WALKS AND WILDLIFE POND

(F.C.)

Route passes through mixed woodland and open moorland via a wildlife pond frequented by geese, mallard and wigeon.
Situation. 5 miles north-east of Fettercairn, 3 miles east of B974. O.S. 1" map sheet 40, ref. NO 696798.

Ke.3. ST CYRUS NATURE RESERVE

(N.C.C.)

227 acres of land between cliff and high water mark. The rich basalt cliffs, sand dunes and salt marsh north of the mouth of the River North Esk support many plants near the northern limit of their range in Britain. Research and management are directed towards protecting these plant communities by controlling spread of gorse and bracken and fires. A 1½ mile Nature Trail identifies much of the wildlife of this coastal habitat.
Nature Trail booklet 3p obtainable on reserve. Assistant Regional Officer, Nature Conservancy Council, Brathens, Banchory, Kincardineshire. Telephone 2206.

KINROSS-SHIRE Map 5

Ks.1. Loch Leven, CASTLE *(P.S.A.)*

The tower is of late 14th or early 15th century date. Mary Queen of Scots
was imprisoned in the castle in 1567 and from it escaped a year later.

*Situation. On an island in Loch Leven. O.S. 1" map sheet 55,
ref. NO 138018.*

*Admission. Kinross Town Council ferry service: Adult 15p, child 5p (under
14 years of age). Free admission to castle. Daily in summer only,
except Sundays, 10-6. Sundays 2-6. Leaflet 1p.*

Loch Leven, FINDATIE PICNIC SITE *(Perth & Kinross Joint CC)*

Large car park with access to south shore of loch.

LOCH LEVEN NATURE RESERVE *(N.C.C.)*

This loch, besides being world famous for its trout fishing, is also the most
important fresh-water area in Britain for migratory and breeding wildfowl.
Much scientific research is carried out at the loch. In autumn thousands of
geese arrive at Loch Leven and later disperse over Scotland. Many thousands
of duck winter on the loch, and those which breed include mallard, tufted duck,
gadwall, teal and shoveler. Public access is allowed only at three points on the
shore—Kinross (Kirkgate Park), Findatie (near the RSPB's Vane Farm Nature
Centre) and Burleigh Sands – and to Castle Island.

Warden: A. Allison, Benarty, The Vane, near Kinross.

LOCH LEVEN NATURE CENTRE *(R.S.P.B.)*

The first Nature Centre to be established in the U.K. Situated at Vane Farm
Nature Reserve on south shores of Loch Leven. Between last week of
September and April, the area is a favourite feeding and resting place for
vast numbers of wild geese and duck. The Centre itself is a converted farm
building equipped with displays designed to interpret the surrounding
countryside and the Loch. There is also a Nature Trail leading to the top of
Vane Hill. A qualified teacher/warden instructs (by appointment) organised
parties of schoolchildren in conservation education.

*Access. Open to visitors from 9.30-5.30 every day except Fridays.
Car park, picnic site and toilets available.*

Ks.2. Milnathort, BURLEIGH CASTLE *(P.S.A.)*

A fine tower-house dating from about 1500, roofless but otherwise almost
intact. The castle was several times visited by James VI.

*Situation. ½ mile east of Milnathort on the Leslie road. O.S. 1" map sheet
53, ref. NO 130047.*

*Admission. All reasonable times without charge on application to key-keeper
at farm opposite.*

KIRKCUDBRIGHTSHIRE Maps 1, 2 & 4

CAERLAVEROCK (See Dumfriesshire)

Kir.1.   Castle Douglas, THREAVE CASTLE   *(P.S.A.)*
This mighty tower of the "Black Douglases" was built towards the end of
the 14th century, and dismantled after its capture by the Covenanters in 1640.
*Situation. 1½ miles west of Castle Douglas. Access by farm road from road
to Gatehouse of Fleet (A75). O.S. 1" map sheet 81, ref. NX 739623.
Admission. Open all year except when ferry is being serviced. 5p (includes
ferry charge). Official Guide Pamphlet 1p.*

Castle Douglas, THREAVE GARDENS   *(N.T.S.)*
Used as a training centre for young gardeners.
*Admission 25p, children 5p. Open daily all year. Gardens 9-sunset; walled
garden and glasshouses 9-5. Guide book 10p.*

Castle Douglas, THREAVE WILDFOWL REFUGE   *(N.T.S.)*
Screened viewpoints where geese and duck can be observed. Conducted
tours (free to members of The National Trust for Scotland) in parties up to 10
daily except Monday by previous arrangement with warden. Access: November-
March.
*Limited car parking. Free leaflet (N.T.S.); Warden, Mr J. McNish, Kelton Mill
(Tel. Bridge of Dee 242) and N.T.S., Threave House, Castle Douglas (Tel. 2575)*

Kir.2.   Corsock, KNOWETOP LOCHS NATURE RESERVE   *(S.W.T.)*
Two small lochs together with a wide range of typical upland habitats
traversed by a nature trail. Permits are required except on open days, when
the public will be particularly welcomed, and are available from the
*Hon. Warden, Mr R. F. Stewart, Knowetop, Corsock, Stewartry of Kirkcudbright.
A leaflet describing the Reserve is available from the Warden (10p).
Situation. 3 miles NW of Corsock on Dumfries-New Galloway road.
O.S. 1" map sheet 74, ref NX 706786.*

Kir.3.   Creetown, CAIRN HOLY   *(P.S.A.)*
Two cairns which belong to the Galloway group of Clyde-Carlingford
chambered tombs, yielding both Neolithic pottery and Beaker fragments.
*Situation. 4 miles south-east of Creetown, off the road to Gatehouse of Fleet.
O.S. 1" map sheet 80, ref. NX 518541.
Admission. All times without charge.*

Creetown, CARSLUITH CASTLE   *(P.S.A.)*
A roofless 16th century tower-house on the L-plan, which differs from most
buildings of this class in that the staircase wing is an addition, dated 1568.
*Situation. 3 miles south-south-east of Creetown, on the road to Gatehouse
of Fleet. O.S. 1" map sheet 80, ref. NX 495542.
Admission. All reasonable times without charge, on application to custodian.
Leaflet.*

Kir.4. Dalbeattie, MOTE OF MARK   *(N.T.S.)*

An ancient hill fort on the estuary of the river Urr at Rockcliffe. Held by the
National Trust for Scotland since 1937, it overlooks Rough Island,
another Trust property maintained as a bird sanctuary. Adjacent, too, are
Muckle Lands and Jubilee Path, a stretch of coastline between Rockcliffe and
Kippford, in the care of the Trust.

Accessible at all times. Rough Island can be reached on foot at low tide.

Kir.5. Dumfries, MABIE FOREST TRAILS   *(F.C.)*

Excellent views of surrounding country and the Solway coast can be obtained
from the walks. Car park and picnic place.

Booklets available at start of walks (12p).
Situation. About 5 miles south-west of Dumfries. O.S. 1" map sheet 74, ref.
NY 949712.

Dumfries, SWEETHEART ABBEY   *(P.S.A.)*

Founded in 1273 in memory of John Balliol (of Balliol College, Oxford).
This beautiful ruin has a precinct wall built of enormous boulders.

Situation. At New Abbey, 6 miles south of Dumfries on the coast road.
O.S. 1" map sheet 74, ref. NX 965663.
Admission. Standard. 5p. Official Guide Book 9p.

Kir.6. GALLOWAY FOREST PARK   *(F.C.)*

Situated in the heart of Galloway, this Forest Park holds the best of the
south-west's magnificent scenery of crag, fell, torrent and loch. Loch Trool
Forest Walk (four miles) leads through an area closely associated with Robert
the Bruce and past a memorial stone recording his victory over the English
in the Battle of Glen Trool (AD 1307).
Forest Walks: Larg Hill and Bruntis Forest Trail (Booklet 10p) — Trail starts
at Daltamie Forest Nursery, Kirroughtree Forest, and leads to a scenic viewpoint
overlooking Bruntis Loch.
Situation. 3 miles south-east of Newton Stewart on A75.
Loch Trool Forest Trail (Guide 10p) — This leads round Loch Trool through
mixed woodland including famous sessile oakwoods (designated by the
Nature Conservancy as a Site of Special Scientific Interest) and past the Steps
of Trool, site of Bruce's famous battle.
Situation. Caldon's F.C. camp site at the west end of Loch Trool.
Stroan Bridge Forest Walk (Booklet 10p) — Walk starts and ends at Stroan
Bridge car park 1 mile east of Glen Trool village on A174.
Talnotry Forest Trail (Booklet 10p) — Walk starts from opposite Talnotry F.C.
camp site ½ mile south of Murray's Monument.
Situation. On A712 Newton Stewart-New Galloway road.
Wild Goat Park: a herd of feral or wild goats can be seen in the Goat Park
near Talnotry on A712, 7 miles north-east of Newton Stewart.
Galloway Deer Museum: on A712 beside Clatteringshaws Loch.

Booklets from Forestry Commission Warden's shop at Caldon's Camp, Glen
Trool, and Talnotry Camp, Kirroughtree.

STROAN BRIDGE PICNIC SITE   *(Kirkcudbright C.C./F.C.)*

Picnic area 1 mile east of Glentrool village; starting point for Stroan Bridge
Forest Walk.

Kir.7. Gatehouse of Fleet, CARDONESS CASTLE *(P.S.A.)*

A well-preserved 15th century tower-house. The fireplaces in the great hall and the upper hall or solar are particularly good.
Situation. 1 mile south-west of Gatehouse of Fleet, on the main road to Newton Stewart. O.S. 1" map sheet 73, ref. NX 591553.
Admission. Standard. 5p.

Gatehouse of Fleet, MURRAY FOREST CENTRE *(F.C.)*

Log cabin type building in the Fleet Forest, with information centre, picnic sites and car park. Three walks, within easy distance of the centre, serve to demonstrate some of the forester's work. Booklet 7p from Forest Office, Gatehouse of Fleet, or honesty box at start of walks.
Situation. About ½ mile south-east of Gatehouse of Fleet.
O.S. 1" map sheet 80, ref. NX 605562.

Kir.8. Kirkcudbright, DHOON SHORE PICNIC SITE *(Kirkcudbright C.C.)*

A picnic place beside the B727 road near Gull Craig with access to the shore of Kirkcudbright Bay.

Kir.9. Kirkcudbright, DUNDRENNAN ABBEY *(P.S.A.)*

This Cistercian house was founded in 1142. The ruins include much late Norman and Transitional work.
Situation. Dundrennan, 6½ miles south-east of Kirkcudbright.
O.S. 1" map sheet 81, ref. NX 749475.
Admission. Standard. 5p. Official Guide Pamphlet 1p.

Kir.10. Kirkcudbright, MACLELLAN'S CASTLE *(P.S.A.)*

This handsome castellated mansion, built after 1577 is elaborately planned and its architectural details are particularly fine. It has been a ruin since 1752.
Situation. In the centre of Kirkcudbright. O.S. 1" map sheet 80, ref. NX 683511.
Admission. Standard. 10p. Leaflet 1p.

Kir.11. Kirkgunzeon, DRUMCOLTRAN TOWER *(P.S.A.)*

A good example of a Scottish tower-house of about the middle of the 16th century. It is simple and severe.
Situation. Among farm buildings, 4½ miles north-east of Dalbeattie, west of the Dumfries road. O.S. 1" map sheet 81, ref. NX 869683.
Admission. All times without charge. Leaflet.

Kir.12. Lauriston, WOODHALL LOCH PICNIC SITE *(Kirkcudbright C.C.)*

Picnic place beside the A762 road about 2 miles north of Lauriston, and adjacent to Woodhall Loch.

Kir.13. Palnackie, ORCHARDTON TOWER *(P.S.A.)*

An example, unique in Scotland, of a tower house of cylindrical form. It was built by John Cairns about the middle of the 15th century.
Situation. At Old Orchardton, 5½ miles south-east of Castle Douglas.
O.S. 1" map sheet 81, ref. NX 817551.
Admission. All reasonable times without charge, on application to custodian at nearby cottage. Leaflet.

LANARKSHIRE Maps 4 & 5

La.1. Biggar, COULTER MOTTE HILL *(P.S.A.)*

A good example of an early medieval castle mound, originally moated and probably surmounted by a palisade enclosing a timber tower.

Situation. At Coulter railway station. O.S. 1" map sheet 68, ref. NT 019363.
Admission. All times without charge.

Biggar, GLADSTONE COURT MUSEUM *(Biggar Museum Trust)*

Items from Biggar and the surrounding district, representing the period 1800-1914, are shown in this small "street" museum. Grocer, ironmonger, druggist, photographer, bootmaker, watchmaker and printer are among the trades and crafts illustrated by shops and workrooms. The museum also includes a schoolroom, bank and telephone exchange.

Situation. In Biggar behind Lambies (Ironmongers) shop.
Admission. May-October, daily 10-12.30, 2-5 (except Wednesday afternoons, Sunday mornings and local holidays). Adults 10p, children 5p. Leaflets.

La.2. Bellshill, ORBISTON GLEN NATURE TRAIL

This 1¾ mile trail follows the west bank of the South Calder Water. A "four seasons" booklet encourages children to observe the varied wildlife along the trail and to identify it with the help of keys. The area has historical associations with Robert Owen, the social reformer.

Booklet 10p obtainable from Director, Strathclyde Park, Raith Cottage, Bothwellhaugh Road, Bothwell.

La.3. Crawfordjohn, CLEUCH PICNIC SITE *(Lanark CC)*

Picnic area beside the Duneaton Water, off B740 about 2 miles from its junction with A74.

La.4. Douglas, ST BRIDE'S CHURCH *(P.S.A.)*

All that remains of this church is the unaisled choir and the south side of the nave. The choir contains three fine altar-tombs of the great Douglas family.

Situation. In Douglas, on the Edinburgh-Cumnock road.
O.S. 1" map sheet 68, ref. NS 835311.
Admission. All reasonable times without charge, on application to custodian. Leaflet.

La.5. Glasgow, DAWSHOLM PARK NATURE TRAIL *(Glasgow Corporation)*
This trail is designed to assist children to think about and look at living things, making discoveries for themselves.
Guidebook 7p from Parks Department, 20 Trongate, Glasgow.
(Teachers and party leaders should contact the Superintendent, Dawsholm Park, Ilay Road, Glasgow G61 1QQ. Telephone 041-942 4336.)

Glasgow, KELVINGROVE NATURE TRAIL   *(Glasgow Corporation)*

Written primarily for children, the booklet encourages them to follow lines of investigation and discovery.

Guide book 7p from Information Counter, Museum and Art Galleries, Kelvingrove; or Park Superintendent, Sunlight Cottage G11 6PB. Telephone 041-339 3416.

Glasgow, LINN PARK NATURE TRAIL   *(Glasgow Corporation)*

"Four Seasons" Nature Trail, designed for use by school parties and encouraging children to look, discover and use the identification keys, has a guidebook in four seasonal sections covering all aspects of natural history within the park. Riverside walks, pine and deciduous woodlands, historical association, nature centre.

Guide book 10p from Parks Department, 20 Trongate, Glasgow. (Teachers and party leaders should contact the Superintendent, Linn Park, Cathcart, Glasgow G44 5TA. Telephone 041-637 3096).

Glasgow, POLLOCK PARK NATURE TRAILS   *(Glasgow Corporation)*

Two trails interpret woodland and riverside features with the aid of guide sheets.* Helpful for adults or children wanting to know more about the inter-relationship of living things. Over 300 acres of woodland.

*Sheets free from Parks Department, 20 Trongate, Glasgow G1 5ES or Superintendent, 57 Haggs Road, Glasgow G41 4RD.

Glasgow, ROSSHALL PARK TRAIL   *(Glasgow Corporation)*

The woodland and garden trails encourage children to discover facts for themselves and to learn about the influence of Man on nature.

Guide book 7p from Parks Department, 20 Trongate, Glasgow; or Park Information Centre, 161 Crookston Road, Glasgow G52 3NQ. Telephone 041-882 3554.

Glasgow, SPRINGBURN PARK NATURE TRAIL   *(Glasgow Corporation)*

A discovery trail for children of all ages designed to make them aware of the effect of man on his environment.

Guide book 7p from Parks Department, 20 Trongate, Glasgow G1 5ES; or Information Hut, Balgray Hill, Glasgow G21 3AX. Telephone 041-558 5364.

Glasgow, WALKWAYS   *(Glasgow Corporation)*

A system of pedestrian walkways, linking up the major open spaces in the city and leading outwards to adjacent countryside, is in process of development. To date, four sections have been opened: River Cart Walkway includes Ross Hall and Lochar Parks and provides riverside walks and children's play area. Victoria Park Walkway includes an informal walk and a children's kick-about area.
Levern Walkway incorporates Househill Park and will eventually be linked to the proposed Country Park area of Darnley.
River Kelvin Walkway, part of a larger scheme which will link Kelvingrove Park to the nearby countryside.

La.6. Hamilton, NEILSLAND PARK NATURE TRAIL   *(Burgh of Hamilton)*
The aim of the trail is to draw attention to some of the plant life in a
woodland area and in particular to study the life history of trees.
Booklet 5p from Burgh of Hamilton Parks Department.

Hamilton, STRATHCLYDE PARK
Development of this proposed country park in the Clyde Valley is now well
under way. The facilities to be provided include nature reserves, a large new
loch for water sports, picnic areas and camping sites.

La.7. Lanark, COREHOUSE (FALLS OF CLYDE) NATURE RESERVE
(S.W.T.)

Woodland reserve, with wide variety of plants, birds and animals, on the
outskirts of Lanark. Permit required — obtainable from *Reserve Secretary,
Mrs I. Beal, 18 Ladyacre Road, Lanark* — except on certain open days, which
will be notified in the local press, and on which the public will be particularly
welcomed. Entry for visitors to the Reserve is by the West Lodge of
Corehouse where there is space for car parking.
*A booklet describing the Reserve, its wildlife and two nature trails, is
available from the Secretary, price 15p plus postage.*

Lanark, CRAIGNETHAN CASTLE   *(P.S.A.)*
This well-preserved ruin, famous as the "Tillietudlem" of Scott's *Old Mortality,*
has a history of much importance in the religious wars of the 16th century.
*Situation. 4½ miles west-north-west of Lanark, on the west bank of the
River Nethan. O.S. 1" map sheet 61, ref. NS 815463.*
Admission. Standard. 5p. Leaflet.

La.8. Uddingston, BOTHWELL CASTLE   *(P.S.A.)*
This was the largest and finest stone castle in Scotland dating from before
the War of Independence, later reconstructed by the Douglases.
*Situation. ¾ mile south-west of Uddingston. O.S. 1" map sheet 60,
ref. NS 688593.*
Admission. Standard. 5p. Official Guide Book 9p.

MIDLOTHIAN

Mi.1.   East Calder, ALMONDELL AND CALDERWOOD COUNTRY PARK
(Midlothian C.C.)

☆
⌂
👣

The Almondell section of the park covers 90 acres of wooded estate, river
and canal; the Calderwood section is 130 acres of open countryside. There
are picnic areas and a nature trail in the park and footpaths lead from it to
Lin's Mill and to Livingston New Town.
*Situation. Immediately to the NE (Almondell) and S (Calderwood) of Mid
Calder. Access to both sections from A767 at Mid Calder; other entrances to
Almondell section from A71 at East Calder and via minor road (2 miles)
signposted on A8 at Broxburn.*
*Free leaflet about Park; nature trail booklet "Man and Almondell" 10p; from
Park Ranger, Tony Anthony, 81 Mansfield, East Calder.*

Mi.2.   Edinburgh, CRAIGMILLAR CASTLE   *(P.S.A.)*

🏰

This renowned castle is associated with some of the most tragic episodes in
the career of Queen Mary. It has a central 14th century tower.
*Situation. 2½ miles south-east of central Edinburgh, to the east of the
Edinburgh-Dalkeith road. O.S. 1" map sheet 62, ref. NT 285710.*
Admission. Standard. 10p. Official Guide Book 11p.

Edinburgh, CRAMOND VILLAGE WALKWAYS   *(Edinburgh Corporation)*

👣

From this picturesque village on the Firth of Forth walkways lead along the
wooded banks of the River Almond to the Old Cramond Bridge, and along the
seafront to Silverknowes and Granton. Cramond was originally a Roman fort,
"Caer Almond" — Fort on the Almond, which was built about AD 142 by the
Roman Emperor, Antoninus Pius.

Edinburgh, HERMITAGE AND BLACKFORD NATURE TRAIL
(Edinburgh Corporation)

👣

Nature trail from gates of Hermitage of Braid Public Park (off Braid Road)
via the summit of Blackford Hill, about two hours.
The trail booklet by using keys, diagrams and questions, involves children
from urban school groups in a variety of wildlife habitats and places of
industrial and historical interest.
Booklet 5p from Edinburgh Corporation, Education Department.

Mi.3.   Musselburgh, INVERESK LODGE GARDEN   *(N.T.S.)*

❀

With its interest in the Lodge, an attractive 17th century house in one of the
most unspoiled villages in the Lothians, the Trust has worked closely with the
local Inveresk Preservation Society who have been markedly successful in
their efforts to retain the existing overall character of the village.
*Admission. The Lodge is let to a tenant and is not normally open to the public.
The garden, however, is open all year, Monday-Friday 10-4.30; also Sundays,
May-September 2-5. Adult 20p, children accompanied by adult, free.*

Mi.4.   Pathhead, CRICHTON CASTLE   *(P.S.A.)*

🏰

One of the largest and finest of Scottish castles with a plain 14th century
tower-house as nucleus. Other stone work is in the Italianate manner.
*Situation. 2¼ miles south-south-west of Pathhead which is on the
Edinburgh-Lauder road. O.S. 1" map sheet 62, ref. NT 380612.*
Admission. Standard, but closed on Fridays, October-May. 5p.
Official Guide Book 14p.

MIDLOTHIAN

Mi.5.　Penicuik, CASTLE LAW FORT　*(P.S.A.)*
A small Iron Age hill fort consisting of two concentric banks and ditches.
In the older rock-cut ditch a souterrain or earth-house is preserved.
Situation. On the summit of Castle Knowe, a small hill on the south-eastern
slopes of the Pentland Hills, west of the Edinburgh-Carlops road, about
1 mile north-west of Glencorse. O.S. 1" map sheet 62, ref. NT 229639.
Admission. Without charge. May be viewed from outside. Permission to
enter by prior application only to the Department of the Environment,
Argyle House, 3 Lady Lawson Street, Edinburgh EH3 9SD. Leaflet.

Mi.6.　SLATEFORD-JUNIPER GREEN-BALERNO RAILWAY WALK
(Edinburgh Corporation & Midlothian C.C.)
A walkway along the former Balerno Branch railway line and adjoining the
wooded Dells of Colinton and Craiglockhart. The Slateford-Juniper Green
section forms a major link in the City's proposed Water of Leith Walkway and
joins Midlothian County Council's railway walk leading on out of town to
Balerno.
Leaflet from Edinburgh Corporation Planning Department.

ISLANDS

Mi.7.　INCHMICKERY NATURE RESERVE　*(R.S.P.B.)*
Formerly an important breeding island for terns. Measures were instituted
in 1972 to control the ever increasing gull population which has been
ousting the terns in recent years.
Access. By permit only from R.S.P.B. Scottish Office, 17 Regent Terrace,
Edinburgh EH7 5BN. Telephone 031-556 5624.

MORAYSHIRE

Mo.1. Burghead, ROSEISLE PICNIC SITE *(F.C.)*
Woodland picnic area with access to coast and beach. Reached from the
B9089 road about 3½ miles south of Burghead.

Burghead, WELL *(P.S.A.)*
This remarkable rock-cut structure is probably an early Christian baptistery.
Situation. At Burghead, 8 miles north-west of Elgin.
O.S. 1" map sheet 29, ref. NJ 110692.
Admission. All times without charge. Leaflet.

Mo.2. Duffus, CASTLE *(P.S.A.)*
The finest example of a motte and bailey castle in the north of Scotland,
unique by reason of the wide outer precinct ditch which surrounds the castle.
Situation. At Old Duffus, 3 miles north-west of Elgin.
O.S. 1" map sheet 29, ref. NJ 189673.
Admission. All times without charge. Official Guide Pamphlet 2½p.
(Available at Elgin Cathedral and St Peter's Church Duffus.)

Duffus, ST PETER'S CHURCH AND PARISH CROSS *(P.S.A.)*
Duffus Church retains the base of a 14th century-tower and a vaulted porch
of the 16th century. The Cross is apparently of 14th century date.
Situation. In Duffus churchyard, 4½ miles north-west of Elgin.
O.S. 1" map sheet 29, ref. NJ 175687.
Admission. All times without charge.

Mo.3. Elgin, "BISHOP'S HOUSE" *(P.S.A.)*
A small remnant of what is by tradition the town house of the Bishops of
Moray immediately opposite Elgin Cathedral.
Situation. North-west of Elgin Cathedral. O.S. 1" map sheet 29,
ref. NJ 222631.
Admission. Not yet open to the public.

Elgin, CATHEDRAL *(P.S.A.)*
When entire, this was perhaps the most beautiful of our Scottish cathedrals.
It was founded in 1224; but in 1390 was burned by the "Wolf of Badenoch".
Situation. In Elgin. O.S. 1" map sheet 29, ref. NJ 223630.
Admission. Standard. 10p. Official Guide Book 9p.

Mo.4. Elgin, MILLBUIES PICNIC SITE *(Moray and Nairn Joint C.C.)*
Picnic area and woodland walk reached from A941 road about 4 miles south
of Elgin.

Mo.5. Elgin, MONAUGHTY FOREST WALKS *(F.C.)*
Four forest walks, car park, picnic area, toilets. (Joint scheme with Moray
County Council.)
Situation. 4 miles south-west of Elgin on way to Pluscarden Abbey. O.S. 1"
map sheet 29, ref. NJ 164587.

MORAY AND NAIRN

Mo.6. Fochabers, SPEYMOUTH FOREST WALKS   *(F.C.)*

Winding Walks. Fine view of Speyside and Moray Coast from "Peep's View"
gazebo. Car park, picnic area.
*Situation. 1 mile east of Fochabers on A98. O.S. 1" map sheet 30, ref.
NJ 358587.*
Allt Dearg Forest Walk. River walk 1½ miles due south of Fochabers. Fine
views of turbulent Spey and unique "earth pillars". Car park.

Mo.7. Forres, BRODIE PICNIC SITE   *(R. Masson, Brodie)*

Picnic area with woodland walk. Craft shop and restaurant. On north side of
A96 road 3½ miles west of Forres.

Mo.8. Forres, FINDHORN DUNE PICNIC SITE   *(Moray and Nairn Joint C.C.)*

Picnic area, on north-east side of Findhorn Bay, with access to coast and beach.

Mo.9. Forres, SUENO'S STONE   *(P.S.A.)*

One of the most remarkable early sculptured monuments in Scotland;
20 feet high.
*Situation. At the east end of Forres, beside the road to Kinloss.
O.S. 1" map sheet 29, ref. NJ 047595.
Admission. All times without charge.*

NAIRNSHIRE   Map 9

Na.1. Auldearn, BOATH DOOCOT   *(N.T.S.)*

A 17th century dovecote on Castle Hill. It occupies the site of the ancient
royal castle of Auldearn. Commands a panoramic view of the field of battle
where Montrose, leading Charles 1's forces, defeated the Covenanters in 1645.
*Situation. 2 miles east of Nairn. O.S. 1" map sheet 28, ref. NH 917556.
Battle plan on display. Donations box.*

Na.2. Nairn, ARDCLACH BELL TOWER   *(P.S.A.)*

The two storey tower is dated 1655. The bell summoned the worshippers to
the Parish Church and gave warning to the neighbourhood in cases of alarm.
*Situation. 8½ miles south-east of Nairn, west of the road to
Grantown-on-Spey. O.S. 1" map sheet 29, ref. NH 954453.
Admission. All reasonable times on application to Custodian.*

ORKNEY

Map 13

Note: Monuments on the mainland are easily accessible. The Brough of Birsay site is on a tidal island. There is no crossing by boat. Crossing by foot is impossible in the period approximately 3 hours before High Water to 3 hours after it. High Water is an hour before High Water at Kirkwall, which is intimated at the Harbourmaster's office there. Visitors can enquire about access by telephoning the custodian, Mr Matches, Birsay 272. There is a daily boat to Rousay from Mainland by Mr Magnus Flaws, Telephone Wyre 203, who can arrange for motor-boat transport to Rousay, Egilsay, Eynhallow and Wyre at other times as well. Intending visitors to Rousay should contact the key-keeper of the monuments, Mr Marwick, Telephone Wasbister 4, for motor transport on that island, which has no bus service. A regular steamer operates from Kirkwall and visitors to Sanday, Westray and Holm of Papa Westray should consult the timetable. Hoy is reached by boat from Stromness, operated by Mr Angus Brown, Telephone Stromness 240, and a car can be hired on the island by arrangement with Mr Moar, Telephone Hoy 201. The custodian of the Holm of Papa Westray Cairn is Mr Rendall, Cuppins, Papa Westray, whose boat will be required for the short crossing to the Holm. There is also a daily inter-island air service. For further information visitors should consult Mr Windwick, custodian at the Earl's Palace, Kirkwall. The attention of visitors is drawn to the Official Guide Book to Orkney monuments, obtainable from the Stationery Office and at the principal monuments on the Orkney Mainland. Price 14p.

MAINLAND

Or.1.   Aikerness, THE BROCH OF GURNESS   *(P.S.A.)*

An Iron Age broch tower still standing over 10 feet high surrounded by other buildings, the whole encircled by a deep rock-cut ditch.
Situation. On the coast at Aikerness, near Evie, about 11 miles north-west of Kirkwall and 1½ miles north of the main road (A966).
O.S. 1" map sheet 6, ref. HY 383268.
Admission. Standard, but closed on Saturdays during winter. 5p.
Official Guide Pamphlet 1p.

Or.2.   Birsay, THE BROUGH OF BIRSAY   *(P.S.A.)*

On this tidal island stands a ruined Romanesque church. A magnificent sculptured stone was discovered in the ruins and is now in the National Museum.
Situation. At Birsay, north end of Mainland, 20 miles north-west of Kirkwall.
O.S. 1" map sheet 6, ref. HY 239285.
Admission. All reasonable times, but closed on Mondays in winter.
Crossings by foot except at High Water. No crossing by boat. 5p.
Official Guide Book, "The Early Christian and Norse Settlements, Birsay",
price 9p. (Available at major monuments in Orkney).

Birsay, EARL'S PALACE   *(P.S.A.)*

Extensive but dilapidated ruin of palace built for Robert, Earl of Orkney in 1574. Few details of the interior arrangements can now be identified.
Situation. Near the shore, 1 mile south-east of the Brough of Birsay, at the end of road A966. O.S. 1" map sheet 6, ref. HY 246280.
Admission. All times without charge.

Or.3. Dounby, CLICK MILL (P.S.A.)

The only example of the old Orcadian horizontal water-mills still in working condition.

Situation. 2 miles north-west of Dounby, on B9057. O.S. 1" map sheet 6, ref. HY 325228.
Admission. All times without charge. Official Guide Pamphlet 1p. (Available at Earl's Palace, Kirkwall.)

Or.4. Finstown, CUWEEN HILL CAIRN (P.S.A.)

A mound covering a megalithic passage tomb, the main chamber having four mural cells. Contained the bones of men, dogs and oxen (*c.* 2000 B.C.).

Situation. About ½ mile south of Finstown, which is 6 miles west-north-west of Kirkwall (A965). O.S. 1" map sheet 6, ref. HY 364128.
Admission. All reasonable times without charge, on application to keykeeper at nearby farmhouse.

Finstown, DALE OF COTTASGARTH NATURE RESERVE (R.S.P.B.)

Attractive heather valley with small stream and willow clumps. Breeding ground for hen harrier, merlin, kestrel and short-eared owl.

Situation. 4 miles north of Finstown. O.S. 1" map sheet 6, ref. HY 375200.
Access. By appointment only with Mr David Lea, Easter Sower, Orphir. Telephone Orphir 251.

Or.5. Kirkwall, THE BISHOP'S PALACE (P.S.A.)

An extensive ruin closely adjoining the Cathedral, dating originally from the 12th century, but much altered subsequently.

Situation. In Kirkwall, south of the Cathedral. O.S. 1" map sheet 6, ref. HY 447108.
Admission. See under Earl Patrick's Palace.

Kirkwall, EARL PATRICK'S PALACE (P.S.A.)

This magnificent building has been described as "the most mature and accomplished piece of Renaissance architecture left in Scotland".

Situation. In Kirkwall, south of the Cathedral. O.S. 1" map sheet 6, ref. HY 448108.
Admission. April-September, weekdays 9.30-7, Sundays 2-7. October-March, weekdays, 10-dusk, Sundays 2-dusk. 5p (including Bishop's Palace). Official Guide Book 9p.

Kirkwall, GRAIN EARTH-HOUSE (P.S.A.)

A well-built Iron Age souterrain or earth-house comprising entrance stair, passage and underground chamber; the roof is supported by stone pillars.

Situation. About ¾ mile north-west of Kirkwall, within the boundaries of the old Hatston airfield. O.S. 1" map sheet 6, ref. HY 442117.
Admission. All reasonable times without charge, on application to keykeeper, Mrs D. J. Mitchell, The Shop, Hatston, Kirkwall.

★ **Kirkwall, TANKERNESS HOUSE MUSEUM** *(Kirkwall Town Council)*
The museum exhibition traces the story of man in Orkney from prehistoric times up to the relatively recent past and provides a comprehensive introduction to the County's wealth of ancient monuments.
Admission to both house and garden is free.

Or.6.   Kirkwall, HOBBISTER NATURE RESERVE *(R.S.P.B.)*
This large new reserve has a good cross-section of Orkney birds including birds of prey, seabirds and moorland birds. Access is from the east side of Waulkmill Bay where a minor road leaves the A964 about 5 miles from Kirkwall. No restrictions are planned but visitors should contact the R.S.P.B. Orkney Officer, D. Lea, Easter Sower, Orphir. (Tel. Orphir 251.)

Or.7.   Kirkwall, RENNIBISTER EARTH-HOUSE *(P.S.A.)*
An excellent example of the Orkney type of Iron Age earth-house consisting of a passage and underground chamber with supporting roof-pillars.
Situation. About 4½ miles west-north-west of Kirkwall, on the Finstown road (A965). O.S. 1" map sheet 6, ref. HY 397127.
Admission. All reasonable times without charge, on application to key-keeper in farmhouse.

Kirkwall, WIDEFORD HILL CAIRN *(P.S.A.)*
A megalithic chambered cairn with three concentric walls. The burial chamber with three large cells is entered by a passage (*c.* 1800 B.C.).
Situation. 2½ miles west of Kirkwall, on the west slope of Wideford Hill. O.S. 1" map sheet 6, ref. HY 409122.
Admission. All reasonable times without charge, on application to the key-keeper.

✝ **Or.8.   Orphir, CHURCH AND EARL'S BU** *(P.S.A.)*
The only example of a round church known to have been built in the Middle Ages in Scotland, derived ultimately from the Church of the Holy Sepulchre at Jerusalem. Adjacent may be an Earl's Palace of Viking times.
Situation. 8 miles west-south-west of Kirkwall, on the north shore of Scapa Flow (A964). O.S. 1" map sheet 6, ref. HY 334043.
Admission. All times without charge.

Or.9.   Stromness, MAES HOWE *(P.S.A.)*
The finest megalithic tomb in the British Isles, the masonry being unsurpassed in Western Europe (*c.* 1800 B.C.) plundered in Viking times.
Situation. About 9 miles west of Kirkwall, on the main Stromness road (A965). O.S. 1" map sheet 6, ref. HY 318128.
Admission. April-September, weekdays, all reasonable times, Sundays 2-7. October- March, all reasonable times, Sundays 2-4.
Apply to key-keeper in nearby farmhouse. 5p. Official Guide Pamphlet 1p.

Stromness, RING OF BROGAR *(P.S.A.)*
A magnificent circle of upright stones with enclosing ditch spanned by causeways (*c.* 1600 B.C.).
Situation. Between Loch of Harray and Loch of Stenness, on road B9055, about 4 miles north-east of Stromness. O.S. 1" map sheet 6, ref. HY 294134.
Admission. All times without charge.

Stromness, STONES OF STENNESS *(P.S.A.)*
The remains of a stone circle standing on a mound or platform encircled by a ditch and bank (*c.* 1800 B.C.).
Situation. On the southern shore of Loch of Harray, on route B9055, about 4 miles north-east of Stromness. O.S. 1" map sheet 6, ref. HY 306126.
Admission. All times without charge.

Or.10.   Stromness, SKARA BRAE: PREHISTORIC VILLAGE   *(P.S.A.)*
An impressive cluster of dwellings preserved in drift sand. The dwellings are amazingly conserved with their stone furniture, hearths and drains (*c.* 1600 B.C.).
Situation. Bay of Skaill, on the west coast, about 6 miles north-north-west of Stromness (B9056). O.S. 1" map sheet 6, ref. HY 231188.
Admission. Standard. 10p. Official Guide Book 14p.

Or.11.   Stromness, UNSTAN, OR ONSTAN, CAIRN   *(P.S.A.)*
An almost circular mound bounded by three concentric walls and covering a megalithic burial chamber divided by slabs into five compartments (*c.* 2500 B.C.).
Situation. About 2½ miles north-east of Stromness,on the Kirkwall road (A965). O.S. 1" map sheet 6, ref. HY 283117.
Admission. All reasonable times without charge, on application to key-keeper.

OTHER ISLANDS

Or.12.   Copinsay, NATURE RESERVE   *(R.S.P.B.)*
The James Fisher Memorial Island has superb seabird cliffs as well as sandy bays on two holms joined to the main island at low tide. An Information Room is available for visitors.
Access. Contact the R.S.P.B. Orkney Officer, David Lea, Easter Sower, Orphir. Tel. Orphir 251.

Or.13.   Egilsay, ST MAGNUS CHURCH   *(P.S.A.)*
This remarkable structure has a tall, cylindrical western tower. A church existed here in 1116 when St Magnus was martyred in or near the building.
Situation. On the island of Egilsay. O.S. 1" map sheet 6, ref. HY 466304.
Admission. All reasonable times without charge, key from nearby farmhouse.

Or.14.   Eynhallow, CHURCH   *(P.S.A.)*
A 12th century church, consisting of nave, chancel and west porch, all greatly altered and now much ruined.
Situation. On the island of Eynhallow. O.S. 1" map sheet 6, ref. HY 359289.
Admission. All times without charge.

Or.15.   Hoy, DWARFIE STANE   *(P.S.A.)*
A burial chamber quarried in a block of sandstone resembling the rock-cut chambered tombs common in the Mediterranean but unique in the British Isles (*c.* 1800 B.C.).
Situation. On the island of Hoy. O.S. 1 " map sheet 6, ref. HY 244005.
Admission. All times without charge. Access by boat from Stromness.

Or.16.   Rousay, BLACKHAMMER CAIRN   *(P.S.A.)*
A long cairn bounded by a retaining wall and containing a megalithic burial chamber divided into seven compartments or stalls (*c.* 2000 B.C.).
Situation. On the south coast of the island, north of B9064.
O.S. 1" map sheet 6, ref. HY 414276.
Admission. All reasonable times without charge.

Rousay, KNOWE OF YARSO CAIRN   *(P.S.A.)*
An oval cairn with concentric walls enclosing a megalithic chambered tomb divided by paired upright slabs into three compartments (*c.* 2000 B.C.).
Situation. On the south coast of the island, north of B9064.
O.S. 1" map sheet 6, ref. HY 403281.
Admission. All reasonable times without charge.

Rousay, MIDHOWE BROCH *(P.S.A.)*

An Iron Age broch tower and walled enclosure situated on a promontory cut off by a deep rock-cut ditch. The enclosure contains secondary buildings.
Situation. On the west coast of the island. O.S. 1" map sheet 6, ref. HY 371308.
Admission. All reasonable times without charge.

Rousay, MIDHOWE CAIRN *(P.S.A.)*

A megalithic chambered tomb in an oval barrow with three concentric walls. The chamber is divided into 12 compartments (*c.* 2000 B.C.).
Situation. On the west coast of the island, close to Midhowe Broch. O.S. 1" map sheet 6, ref. HY 372306.
Admission. All reasonable times without charge.

Rousay, TAVERSOE TUICK CAIRN *(P.S.A.)*

A megalithic chambered burial mound containing two burial chambers divided into stalls (*c.* 2000 B.C.).
Situation. On the south coast of the island north of road B9064. O.S. 1" map sheet 6, ref. HY 426276.
Admission. All reasonable times without charge.

Or.17. Sanday, QUOYNESS CAIRN *(P.S.A.)*

A megalithic chambered cairn with triple retaining walls containing a passage and main chamber with six beehive cells (*c.* 2000 B.C.).
Situation. At Quoyness on the south coast of the island. O.S. 1" map sheet 5, ref. HY 677378.
Admission. All reasonable times without charge, on application to key-keeper. Island steamer service from Kirkwall.

Or.18. Westray, NOLTLAND CASTLE *(P.S.A.)*

A fine ruin in the Z-plan, remarkable for its tiers of gun-loops. It was built between 1560 and 1573 but never completed.
Situation. ½ mile west-north-west of Pierowall. O.S. 1" map sheet 5, ref. HY 429488.
Application. All reasonable times without charge, on application to custodian. Official Guide Pamphlet 2½p.

Westray, PIEROWALL CHURCH *(P.S.A.)*

A ruin consisting of nave and chancel, the latter canted. There are some finely lettered tombstones.
Situation. At Pierowall. O.S. 1" map sheet 5, ref. HY 438487.
Admission. All times without charge.

Or.19. Westray, TUQUOY CHURCH *(P.S.A.)*

A 12th century church, with nave and chancel, the former lengthened in the later Middle Ages. The chancel has a Romanesque arch and was vaulted.
Situation. Bay of Tuquoy, on the south coast of the island. O.S. 1" map sheet 5, ref. HY 455432.
Admission. All times without charge.

Or.20.   Holm of Papa Westray, CAIRN   *(P.S.A.)*

A megalithic chambered cairn of Neolithic date (*c.* 1800 B.C.).
Engravings occur – rare examples of megalithic art in Scotland.
*Situation. On the east side of the island. O.S. 1" map sheet 5,
ref. HY 509518.*
Admission. All reasonable times without charge, on application to custodian.

Papa Westray, KNAP OF HOWAR   *(P.S.A.)*

The ruins of two stone structures lying side by side, apparently of a domestic
character, resembling the secondary buildings at the Broch of Gurness.
*Situation. West side of island of Papa Westray, near Holland House.
O.S. 1" map sheet 5, ref. HY 483519.*
Admission. All times without charge.

Or.21.   Wyre, COBBIE ROW'S CASTLE   *(P.S.A.)*

Mentioned in the Orkneyinga Saga as Kolbein Hruga's "steinkastala"
(*c.* 1145), this remote structure is probably the earliest authenticated stone
castle in Scotland.
Situation. In the centre of the island. O.S. 1" map sheet 6, ref. HY 442264.
Admission. All times without charge.

Wyre, ST MARY'S CHAPEL   *(P.S.A.)*

This ruinous chapel of the late 12th century is a small rectangular Romanesque
structure of nave and chancel, built of local whinstone.
Situation. Near Cobbie Row's Castle. O.S. 1" map sheet 6, ref. HY 443264.
Admission. All times without charge.

PEEBLESSHIRE

Map 5

Ps.1. Innerleithen, TRAQUAIR HOUSE
(P. Maxwell Stuart, Esq.)

Traquair House, formerly known as Traquair Castle, dates from the
10th century and is the oldest inhabited house in Scotland. Twenty-seven
Scottish and English kings have stayed here. Rich in associations with
Mary Queen of Scots and the Jacobite risings. Many historical treasures on
view including letters, embroideries, books, glass and paintings. Unique
18th century brew house in full working production.
*Admission. 2-5.30 Easter Sunday and Monday (1974 only). All Sundays
from the second Sunday in May-end of September, Spring Bank Holidays,
all Wednesdays and Saturdays in June and daily (except Fridays)
July-September. Individually escorted tours of the house during July, August
and 1st week September, Monday-Thursday and Saturday 10-12.30.*

Ps.2. Peebles, CROSS KIRK
(P.S.A.)

The remains of a Trinitarian Friary, consisting of the nave and west tower.
The foundations of the claustral building have been laid bare.
*Situation. In Peebles. O.S. 1" map sheet 62, ref. NT 250408.
Admission. Standard. Without charge. Key from custodian in nearby house.*

Peebles, NEIDPATH CASTLE
*(The Earl of Wemyss and March
Discretionary Trust)*

After the battle of Dunbar in 1650, Lord Yester garrisoned Neidpath Castle
against Cromwellian forces, surrendering in December 1650. Construction
of the Castle had begun during the 14th Century and Lord Yester
made great alterations to the tower, built the present gateway which bears
the family crest and extended the terrace gardens, traces of which may still
be seen. Purchased by the 1st Duke of Queensberry in 1686,
Neidpath Catle has passed down through several heirs to the present
Earl of Wemyss and March, who has directed much of the recent
work of restoration in the Castle.
*Situation. 1 mile west of Peebles on A72. On the River Tweed.
Admission. Adults 10p, children 5p. Open 10-1 and 2-6 Monday to
Saturday and 1-6 Sunday from the Thursday before Easter to
2nd Sunday in October, when staff available. Small car park.
Dogs only on lead.*

Peebles, ROSETTA PICNIC SITE
(Peebles CC)

Picnic area in the grounds of Rosetta House, on the NW outskirts of Peebles.
Information Room.

Ps.3. Peebles, GLENTRESS FOREST
(F.C.)

Oldest State forest in South of Scotland, 2,360 acres. Largely Sitka spruce,
Douglas fir, Scots pine and larch. Choice of several self-guided walks,
ranging from two to nearly five miles, whose accompanying booklet describes
the forest wildlife. Viewpoint at 1,500 feet. Forest walks start at picnic
site, Glentress Forest Office.
*Situation. 2 miles east of Peebles on A72.
Leaflet, 5p, from Glentress Forest Office, Peebles.*

PERTHSHIRE   Maps 4, 5, 7, 8 & 9

Pe.1.   Aberfeldy, BIRKS OF ABERFELDY   *(Aberfeldy Town Council)*
Nature Trail in celebrated beauty spot. Picnic place.
Leaflet 5p. (Aberfeldy Town Council and Scottish Wildlife Trust.)

Aberfeldy, DRUMMOND HILL FOREST WALKS   *(F.C.)*
Four walks varying from 2½ to 8 miles give the visitor a chance to see some
of the wildlife and learn something of the work of the forester.
*Situation. On A827, 2 miles west of Kenmore, and the walk on north
side of Drummond Hill, 1½ miles west of Fortingall.*

Aberfeldy, STRATHTAY HISTORY TRAILS
(Breadalbane Archaeological Society)
Four archaeological and historical trails radiating from Aberfeldy.
Booklet 20p from Aberfeldy Information Centre and Hotels.

Pe.2.   Aberfoyle, INCHMAHOME PRIORY   *(P.S.A.)*
This beautifully situated monastic house is famous as the retreat of the infant
Mary Queen of Scots. It was an Augustinian house, founded in 1238.
*Situation. On an island in the Lake of Menteith, 3 miles east of Aberfoyle.
O.S. 1" map sheet 54, ref. NN 574005.
Access. By ferry from Port of Menteith on request.
Admission 5p. Apri. to mid-November, standard (weather conditions permitting).
From mid-November to 31 March, ferry service has normally to be suspended.
Telephone enquiries to Stirling 3360. Ferry to the island 5p. Official
Guide Pamphlet 1½p.*

Pe.3.   Abernethy, ROUND TOWER   *(P.S.A.)*
One of the two remaining Irish round towers in Scotland (the other is in
Brechin, Angus). It dates from about the end of the 11th century.
*Situation. In Abernethy. O.S. 1" map sheet 55, ref. NO 191165.
Admission. All reasonable times without charge on application to custodian.*

Pe.4.   Auchterarder, TULLIBARDINE CHAPEL   *(P.S.A.)*
This is one of the few Collegiate Churches in Scotland which was entirely
finished and still remains unaltered. It was founded in 1446.
*Situation. 6 miles south-east of Crieff, off the main Auchterarder road.
O.S. 1" map sheet 55, ref. NN 909135.
Admission. All reasonable times without charge, on application to the
key-holder, Mr Maxtone, at adjacent farmhouse. Leaflet.*

Pe.5.   Balquhidder, INVERLOCHLARIG PICNIC SITE   *(Braes Farming Co.)*
Parking and picnic space at the end of the narrow road along the north shores
of Lochs Voil and Doine.

75

Pe.6. BEN LAWERS *(N.T.S.)*

The National Trust for Scotland's property at Ben Lawers covers 8,000 acres
of the southern slopes of the mountain and includes the neighbouring peak
of Ben Ghlas. At 3,984 feet Lawers is the highest mountain in Perthshire
and commands views ranging from the Atlantic to the North Sea and from
the Cairngorms to the Lothians. A direction indicator is mounted in a cairn
at the summit.

The Trust's primary interest in Ben Lawers is the preservation of the remarkable
variety and quantity of alpine flowers which flourish on the cliffs and ledges.
Although the nature trail keeps to the lower slopes it leads through a range
of plant communities including the Alpine zone.

The Trust has co-operated with The Nature Conservancy and the Countryside
Commission for Scotland to establish a visitor centre and exhibition at the
Car Park on the slopes of Ben Ghlas, and to create a National Nature Reserve
in the area.

Admission. Centre open May-September, 10-5.30 daily.
Car park and visitor services 10p. Illustrated book "Ben Lawers and
its Alpine Flowers", 50p, nature trail booklet 10p from N.T.S.
Information Centres at Ben Lawers, Killiecrankie and Dunkeld.
Ranger-Naturalist: Angus McWilliam, (Tel. Killin 397).
Guided walks programme.

Pe.7. BEN LUI NATURE RESERVE *(N.C.C.)*

Ben Lui (3,708 feet) is renowned for its rich montane flora. The mountain
is formed of contrasting rock types of the Dalradian series. The luxuriance of
vegetation on these cliffs and the abundance of herbs in the grassland below
is most striking.

Pe.8. Callander, COILLE BROIN PICNIC SITE *(Perth CC)*

Picnic area with access to shore of Loch Venachar, about 4 miles west of
Callander on A821 road.

Pe.9. Comrie, GLENARTNEY PICNIC SITE *(Drummond Castle Estate)*

Picnic area on south side of the Water of Ruchill, about 6 miles south-west
of Comrie, near the end of a narrow road.

Pe.10. Crianlarich, LOCHDOCHART PICNIC SITE *(Loch Dochart Estate)*

Picnic area and viewpoint beside Loch Dochart, about 2 miles east of
Crianlarich on the A85 trunk road.

Pe.11. Crieff, INNERPEFFRAY CHURCH *(P.S.A.)*

Built in 1508 as a collegiate foundation; it contains an original altar stone,
and part of a small tempera-painted ceiling.
Situation. 3 miles south-east of Crieff, off the Auchterarder road.
O.S. 1" map sheet 55, ref. NN 902185.
Admission. At all reasonable times without charge. Closed on Thursdays.

Crieff, INNERPEFFRAY LIBRARY

Founded almost 300 years ago, though now housed in a late 18th Century
building, this in the oldest public library in Scotland, and contains a large
collection of interesting books.
Situation. Off Crieff-Auchterarder road, 4 miles from Crieff.
Admission. Open daily except Thursdays. May-September weekdays 10-1,
2-5, Sundays 2-4, October-April, weekdays 10-1, 2-4, Sundays 2-4.
Large parties should apply to Librarian, The Schoolhouse, Innerpeffray.
(Crieff 2819).

Pe.12. Crieff, NATURE TRAIL
Along the wooded banks of the River Turret and the lower slopes of the
Knock, a well known local landmark. The trail booklet gives a comprehensive
list of natural features. The lower plants, mosses, liverworts and lichens are
fully described.
Booklet 5p from Crieff Hydro and Crieff Information Centre.

Pe.13. Dunblane, CATHEDRAL   *(P.S.A.)*
The existing building dates mainly from the 13th century. The nave was
unroofed after the Reformation, but the whole building was restored in 1892-5.
Situation. In Dunblane. O.S. 1" map sheet 54, ref. NN 782015.
Admission. Standard, except Sundays in Summer, when 2-5.30.
Without charge.

Pe.14. Dunkeld, CATHEDRAL   *(P.S.A.)*
The choir has been restored and is in use as the parish church. The nave
and the great north-west tower date from the 15th century.
Admission. Standard. 5p. Guidebook 7½p.

Dunkeld, CRAIGVINEAN FOREST WALKS   *(F.C.)*
Car park, picnic area. Walks through mainly coniferous plantations. A short
walk leads to a scenic viewpoint looking up the River Tay.
Situation. On B898 Dunkeld-Aberfeldy road.
Booklet, 10p, which lists the plant and animal life to be seen, from
Dunkeld Forest Office, N.T.S. Information Centre, Dunkeld, and Forestry
Commission, 6 Queen's Gate, Aberdeen AB9 2NQ.

Dunkeld HERMITAGE   *(N.T.S.)*
A woodland pleasance on the River Braan near Inver, the birthplace of the
famous Scottish fiddler Neil Gow (1727-1807). The woods contain some
fine specimens of forest trees and at the Falls of Braan there is the "folly"
known as Ossian's Hall built by a Duke of Atholl in 1758. There is a
woodland walk along the River Braan; sycamore, birch, sitka and Norway
spruce, some of which were planted about 1860, rise to 150 feet.
Accessible at all times but Ossian's Hall closed during winter.
Nature trail booklet 10p from car park at Hermitage and Information Centres
at Dunkeld and Killiecrankie.

Dunkeld, LITTLE HOUSES, AND STANLEY HILL   *(N.T.S.)*
After Culross in Fife the rehabilitation of the heart of old Dunkeld is the most
ambitious and extensive "little houses" restoration scheme undertaken by the
National Trust for Scotland. (in conjunction with Perth C.C.)
Visitor Centre: Easter-mid-October. Mon-Sat. 10-6; Sun 2-6. Guidebook
"Places in Perthshire" 10p. Warden: Mrs N Cassells. Tel. Dunkeld 460.

Pe.15. Enochdhu, Blairgowrie, KINDROGAN FIELD CENTRE   *(S.F.S.A.)*
Established by the Scottish Field Studies Association Ltd. to stimulate interest
in the study of the natural sciences, and the Scottish countryside. Courses
for professional and amateur naturalists.
Kindrogan Field Centre Trail: designed for use by schools at the Centre the
trail endeavours to involve the visitor with the varied wildlife habitats and
also introduces historical detail. *Booklet 8p from Warden.*
Kindrogan Hill Trail: this trail takes the visitor to viewpoints above Kindrogan
from which the topography and land use of Strathardle can be demonstrated.
Booklet 8p from Warden, Mr Brian S. Brookes, B.Sc. Telephone, Strathardle 286.
Situation. Off Moulin-Kirkmichael road.

Pe.16. Fortingall, Garth, YOUTH HOSTEL   *(S.Y.H.A.)*
The hostel at Garth is specially equipped with laboratory and library
facilities for field studies. School parties are welcomed.
(GARTH hostel is at the entrance to Glen Lyon, near Fortingall).
Leaflets from Scottish Youth Hostels Association, 7 Glebe Terrace, Stirling.
FK8 2JA.

Pe.17. Fowlis Wester, SCULPTURED STONE   *(P.S.A.)*
A fine cross-slab, 10 feet high, with Pictish symbols and Celtic enrichment.
The cross is unique in that its arms extend beyond the slab.
Situation. At Fowlis Wester, 4 miles east-north-east of Crieff, to the north
of the Perth road. O.S. 1" map sheet 55, ref. NN 928241.
Admission. All times without charge.

Pe.18. Grandtully, ST MARY'S CHURCH   *(P.S.A.)*
A 16th century church, close to Grandtully Castle, remarkable for its finely
painted wooden ceiling, with heraldic and symbolic subjects.
Situation. At Pitcairn Farm, 2 miles east-north-east of Aberfeldy.
O.S. 1" map sheet 48, ref. NN 886506.
Admission. All times without charge, on application to custodian.

Pe.19. Kinloch Rannoch, CARIE WALKS, RANNOCH FOREST   *(F.C.)*
Forest walks lead from the picnic area on the south side of Loch
Rannoch through open mixed woodland.
Situation. At Carie, 3 miles west of Kinloch Rannoch.

Pe.20. Lochearnhead, GLENOGLEHEAD PICNIC SITE   *(Perth CC)*
Picnic area with viewpoint about 3½ miles north of Lochearnhead on A85 road.

Lochearnhead, LOCH EARNSIDE PICNIC AREAS   *(Perth CC)*
Several picnic areas on north shore of Loch Earn between Lochearnhead and
St. Fillans.

Pe.21. LOCH OF THE LOWES NATURE RESERVE   *(S.W.T.)*
The reserve contains a wide variety of water and woodland birds, plants and
animals. Access to the south shore is unrestricted and there is a visitor centre
and an observation hide at the west end of the loch. Bus parties should
book in advance. Admission to other parts of the Reserve is not
normally allowed.
Situation. Beside Dunkeld-Snaigow road, 3 miles east of Dunkeld.
Booklet 20p at the Visitor Centre, which is open from 10 a.m.-dusk in summer.

Pe.22. Meigle, BELMONT ESTATE NATURE TRAIL   *(City of Dundee)*
A children's trail of discovery, covering many aspects of nature study
and items of interest along the route.
Leaflet 10p from Parks Department, City Square, Dundee, and camp site
at Belmont Estate, Tel. Meigle 246.

Meigle, SCULPTURED STONES   *(P.S.A.)*
These 25 sculptured monuments of the Celtic Christian period, of the
highest artistic and symbolic interest, form a notable assemblage of
Dark Age sculpture.
Situation. At Meigle, on the Coupar Angus-Forfar road.
O.S. 1" map sheet 49, ref. NN 287446.
Admission. Standard, but closed on Sundays. 5p. Official Guide Pamphlet 1p.
The Guide Book of Early Christian and Pictish Monuments is also
available 25p.

Pe.23. Muthill, OLD CHURCH AND TOWER   *(P.S.A.)*
The ruins of an important medieval parish church, mostly early 15th century.
At the west end is a tall Norman tower, once free-standing.
Situation. At Muthill, 3 miles south of Crieff, on the Dunblane road.
O.S. 1" map sheet 55, ref. NN 868171.
Admission. All times without charge.

Pe.24.   PASS OF KILLIECRANKIE   *(N.T.S.)*
The wooded defile is a noted beauty spot with a viewpoint near the head
of the pass. Nearby, where the Garry runs between two great rocks is
the Soldier's Leap. The hero of this is said to have been Donald MacBean,
who served in General Mackay's army at the Battle of Killiecrankie, on
27th July, 1689, which was fought on the hillside a mile north of the Pass.
Mackay led the forces of King William III, and John Graham of Claverhouse
Viscount Dundee, those of James VII. Dundee's Highlanders stripped off
their plaids and footwear and charged to victory, but Dundee himself was
mortally wounded. Part of the Pass, but not the battlefield, is National
Trust for Scotland property.
Trust visitor centre (Tel. Killiecrankie 233) open Easter-mid October,
Mon.-Sat., 10-6; July & August, 9.30-6; Sunday 1-6. Admission. 10p.
(N.T.S. members & children free). Wardens: Mr & Mrs W. H. Ryder,
Old Faskally Cottage (Tel. Killiecrankie 245). Guided walks
programme covers Craigower, Linn of Tummel and Killiecrankie.

Pe.25.   Perth, COUNTRYSIDE TRAIL BY CAR   *(S.W.T.)*
Designed to be read before the motorist sets out, this motor trail describes
many features of interest in Perthshire, and draws together aspects of history,
geology and land-use to explain the appearance of the present-day landscape.
It also contains information about viewpoints, picnic sites, lay-bys and toilets.
Booklet 15p from Perthshire Information Centres and Scottish Wildlife Trust,
8 Dublin Street, Edinburgh.

Perth, ELCHO CASTLE   *(P.S.A.)*
This 16th century fortified mansion survives intact, and is remarkable for its
tower-like "jambs" or wings.
Situation. On the south bank of the Tay, 3½ miles south-east of Perth.
O.S. 1" map sheet 55, ref. NO 164211.
Admission. Standard. 5p. Telephone, Perth 23437. Leaflet.

Pe.26.   Perth, HUNTINGTOWER, OR RUTHVEN CASTLE   *(P.S.A.)*
A castellated mansion of the 15th and 16th centuries remarkable by reason
of its well-preserved painted ceiling.
Situation. 2 miles west of Perth on the Perth-Crieff road. O.S. 1" map
sheet 55, ref. NO 084252.
Admission. Standard. 5p. Official Guide Book 6p.

Pe.27.   Perth, KINNOULL HILL   *(Perth Town Council)*
Nature trail in lovely surroundings on hill which overlooks city. Viewpoint
indicator. Car parking in quarry.
Leaflet (Perth City) from Kiosk, Hatton Road (start of trail); Perth Museum,
City Information Centre, Perth Tourist Association, Marshall Place;
N.T.S. Information Centre, Dunkeld.

Pe.28. Pitlochry, CRAIGOWER (N.T.S.)

An easy, pleasant walk from Pitlochry across the golf course leads to the summit of this modest looking hill above the town. Although only 1,300 feet high it opens up a remarkable variety of vistas, recalling its choice as a beacon hill in earlier times.
Accessible at all times. O.S. 1" map sheet 48, ref. NN 926605.

Pitlochry, DAM & FISH PASS (N.O.S.H.E.B.)

Salmon passing upstream on their way to the spawning grounds can be observed through windows in an underground chamber. Most of the fish pass upstream in late spring and early summer.
Situation. The dam is at the southern end of Loch Faskally and is signposted on the A9. Pitlochry T.C. picnic site.

Pitlochry, DUNFALLANDY STONE (P.S.A.)

An 8th century Pictish cross-slab with a cross, beasts and angels on one side, and with a horseman, seated figures, and Pictish symbols on the other.
Situation. South of Dunfallandy House, 1½ miles south-south-east of Pitlochry. O.S. 1" map sheet 49, ref. NN 946565.
Admission. All times without charge.

Pitlochry, LINN OF TUMMEL NATURE TRAIL (N.T.S.)

A pleasant woodland walk of about 2¼ miles along the right bank of the River Garry leads to the Linn, known as the Falls of Tummel before the water level was raised by the Clunie Hydro-Electric Dam to create Loch Faskally. The trail booklet describes the varied wildlife and the history of the area. Coronation Bridge, about a mile up the Tummel, gives access to an alternative return route to Pitlochry by way of Clunie Power Station.
Accessible at all times. Nature Trail Booklet 10p, Guidebook "Places in Perthshire" 10p, from N.T.S. visitor centres.

Pe.29. Pitlochry, QUEEN'S VIEW FOREST CENTRE & TUMMEL FOREST WALKS (F.C.)

Tummel Forest Centre provides information about the history of the area and describes some of the activities and wildlife of the forest. Variety of F.C. publications on sale.
Situation. Beside the car park leading to the Queen's View, a renowned beauty spot overlooking Loch Tummel. On B8019 road.
Three colour-coded walks of varying length start from the illustrated board at the Clachan Picnic Place and car park ¼ mile west of Queen's View.
Clachan Walk. A short walk which takes in a recently excavated ruined clachan and excellent views of Schiehallion.
Allean Walk. An extension of the Clachan walk through what was formerly known as Allean Forest. Duration – about 2 hours.
Clunie Walk. A longer sign-posted walk of about 3 hours taking in views of Ben y Vrackie and the Clunie Dam at the end of Loch Tummel.
All three walks have a sign-posted diversion to the 'Dun' or 'Ring Fort'.
Faskally Walk is a very attractive walk through mixed woodland of varying ages and along the shore of Loch Dunmore. There are two possible starting points on the A9 road to Blair Atholl, one ½ mile north of Pitlochry, the other at Faskally car park and picnic place near Loch Dunmore ¾ mile north of Pitlochry.
Booklet 'Tummel Forest-Picnic Places and Walks', 10p, from Tummel Forest Office, Queen's View Information Centre, Perthshire Information Centres.

Pe.30. QUEEN ELIZABETH FOREST PARK   *(F.C.)*

The Queen Elizabeth Forest Park extends from the shores of Loch Lomond across the hills to the Trossachs, and holds 25,000 acres of forest land and 20,000 acres of moor and mountains. North of Aberfoyle, the famous "Duke's Road" winds up Craigmore Hill, where the David Marshall Lodge, the F.C.'s picnic pavilion and information centre, (built by the Carnegie Trust) offers magnificent views. Two walks (3 miles and $8\frac{1}{4}$ miles) in Loch Ard Forest and three in Buchanan Forest, Drymen, provide the visitor with an opportunity to see the varied forest wildlife and learn about the work of the forester. Group visits arranged. There are two caravan and camping sites, Cobleland at Aberfoyle, and Cashel between Balmaha and Rowardennan. Youth Hostels are sited at Rowardennan, Kinlochard and Trossachs. All enquiries to Ranger Service, F.C. District Office, Aberfoyle.

Queen Elizabeth Forest Park Guide 60p. Two walks in Loch Ard Forest 10p.
Sallochy and Balmaha Forest Trails 10p.
F.C. publications from David Marshall Lodge, Aberfoyle; Forest Office, Aberfoyle; Camp sites, Cobleland, Aberfoyle; Cashel, Rowardennan.

Pe.31. Strathyre, FOREST CENTRE & WALK   *(F.C.)*

A forest walk starts from a small information centre next to the Strathyre Forest Office on the A84. It follows an old peat extraction road and identifies the variety of trees to be seen along the route.

Pe.32. Thornhill, FLANDERS MOSS NATURE RESERVE   *(S.W.T.)*

Raised bog on deep peat with range of ericaceous and other plants including Cranberry and Andromeda.
Admission by permit obtainable from Trust Secretary, 8 Dublin Street, Edinburgh EH1 3PP. Access by farm track from road B.822 Thornhill to Kippen — $1\frac{3}{4}$ miles south of Thornhill.

RENFREWSHIRE

Map 4

Re.1. Houston, BAROCHAN CROSS *(P.S.A.)*
A fine, free standing Celtic cross, 11 feet high, with figure sculpture.
Not on its original site.
*Situation. 1¼ miles north of Houston, which is 5 miles north-west of the
centre of Paisley. O.S. 1" map sheet 60, ref. NS 406690.*
Admission. All times without charge.

Re.2. Kilbarchan, WEAVER'S COTTAGE *(N.T.S.)*
In summer it is usually possible to see the old craft of handloom weaving
under way at the cottage. Kilbarchan in the 18th century was a thriving
centre of handloom weaving, and the cottage is preserved as a typical weaver's
home of this period.
*Admission. Open Tuesday, Thursday and Saturday (Sunday, May-October
only) 2-5. 15p. Children 5p. Guidebook 10p. Custodian. Mrs H. Munro,
8 Shuttle Street. Trust representative. Mrs A. Halifax-Crawford.*

**Re.3. Lochwinnoch, BARR LOCH AND AIRD MEADOWS NATURE
RESERVE** *(R.S.P.B.)*
This new R.S.P.B. reserve has shallow water with marshy edges and holds
many duck, especially in winter.
*Access. Both Loch and Meadows can be viewed from the A.760 road,
just south-east of the village of Lochwinnoch.*
No further access is allowed unless indicated on the site.

Lochwinnoch, CASTLE SEMPLE COLLEGIATE CHURCH *(P.S.A.)*
The church is a rectangular structure with a remarkable apsidal east end,
each side having three windows of debased Gothic form.
*Situation. At Castle Semple, 1½ miles north-east of Lochwinnoch.
O.S. 1" map sheet 60, ref. NS 376601.*
Admission. Not yet open to the public. May be viewed from the outside.

Re.4. Paisley, PAISLEY GLEN NATURE TRAIL *(Paisley Town Council)*
The Nature Trail is designed to encourage children to look at and
investigate things along the varied route. A booklet in two parts — Spring/
Summer (10p + V.A.T.) and Autumn/Winter (7p + V.A.T.) is available
at the Trail or from the Director of Parks, Municipal Buildings, Paisley.
*The Trail is situated in the Gleniffer Braes Country Park.
There is an Information and Interpretation Unit staffed between the
hours of 8.00 and 16.30. Organised groups should apply in advance to the
Director of Parks, Municipal Buildings, Paisley, PA1 1BU.*

Re.5. RENFREWSHIRE REGIONAL PARK *(Renfrew County Council)*
Lochwinnoch, MUIRSHIEL COUNTRY PARK
Picnic sites, information centre, country trail, junior trail, footpaths into
moorland.
Lochwinnoch, CASTLE SEMPLE LOCH
Water park (200 acre loch) with slipway, pontoon, information centre.
Dinghy sailing, rowing, canoeing, coarse fishing, Winter migrant birds.
Inverkip, CORNALEES BRIDGE
Picnic sites, information centre, walks along "cut" canals (industrial
archaeology) and through hardwood glen.
(Booklets from information centres and County Offices, Paisley.)

ROSS AND CROMARTY

MAINLAND

RC.1. BEINN EIGHE NATURE RESERVE (N.C.C.)

This was the first National Nature Reserve to be declared in Britain, and was acquired primarily for the preservation and study of the fairly large remnant of Caledonian pinewood. The woodlands are being extended within enclosed areas. The mountain slopes of Beinn Eighe are of great geological, physiographical and floristic interest. Pine marten are among the animals protected. Also in the area are wildcat, fox, badger, buzzard, golden eagle. Research work is carried out here from the adjoining Anancaun Field Station. The area displays all the main rocks and there are many Arctic alpine plants. The Glas Leitire Nature Trail takes about 1 hour and starts and finishes at a picnic site on Loch Maree. Proper footwear and warm clothing are essential on the Mountain Trail, which is nearly four miles long and rises to 1,800 feet leading through spectacular scenery. There are picnic and camping areas by Loch Maree near the main road. The Beinn Eighe Information Centre, at Aultroy Cottage near Kinlochewe, will open during the summer of 1974.
Beinn Eighe Nature Reserve pamphlet and trail booklets 3p from Warden.
Details from The Nature Conservancy Council, 12 Hope Terrace, Edinburgh EH9 2AS. Warden. C. Placido, Saltag, Anancaun, Kinlochewe.

RC.2. Braemore, CORRIESHALLOCH GORGE (N.T.S.)

This spectacular mile-long gorge is 200 feet deep, and the Falls of Measach plunge 150 feet. It is visited from Braemore, 12 miles south-east of Ullapool. A suspension bridge provides good viewpoint.
Situation. One mile from Braemore, 12 miles south east of Ullapool on the A.835. O.S. 1" map sheet 20, ref. NH 204777.

Braemore, CORRIESHALLOCH NATURE RESERVE (N.C.C.)

The Reserve is a magnificent example of box-canyon, formed by the cutting back of a river (Abhainn Droma) through hard, horizontally disposed rocks. The tree growth in the walls is generally scanty and dwarfed, except the upper levels, the principal species being wych elm, birch, hazel, sycamore, Norway maple and beech. The plant communities, including certain mosses, are of much interest.
Situation. Near Braemore on the Garve-Ullapool road. Pamphlet, "North West Scotland National Nature Reserves" (available as for Allt nan Carnan leaflet).

Braemore, LAEL FOREST GARDEN AND WALK (F.C.)

This forest arboretum within Lael Forest contains examples of many interesting introduced species. A walk, offering extensive views of the Glen and Loch Broom, climbs the hill behind the garden.
Leaflet 5p from Forest Office and locally.
Situation. On A835 9 miles south-east of Ullapool.

RC.3. Cromarty, HUGH MILLER'S COTTAGE (N.T.S.)

The birthplace of Hugh Miller (1802-56), geologist, naturalist, theologian and writer. The son of a sailing-ship master, Miller became a journeyman stonemason and through natural powers of observation and deduction rose to eminence in the science of geology. The *Old Red Sandstone, The Cruise of the Betsey* and *My Schools and Schoolmasters* are among the most notable of his books. The remarkable variety of his achievement is illustrated at the cottage in his collections of geological specimens, his writings and his personal belongings.
Admission. April-October 10-12, 2-5; Sundays 2-5 June-September only. Adults 10p, children under 12 accompanied by adults free. Guidebook 20p. Custodian. Mrs K. Morrison, Lydia Cottage, Cromarty, Tel. Cromarty 245.

RC.4. Fortrose, CATHEDRAL AND PRECINCTS (P.S.A.)

Such portions of the cathedral as exist are complete, including the vaulting overhead, and there is much fine detail to be seen of 14th century date.
Situation. In Fortrose. O.S. 1" map sheet 28, ref. NH 728565. Admission. All reasonable times without charge, on application to custodian.

RC.5. INVEREWE (N.T.S.)

The Highland garden of Inverewe was created by the redoubtable laird, Osgood Mackenzie, just over a hundred years ago and developed by his daughter, the late Mrs Mairi T. Sawyer. After the bleak, boulder-strewn, landscape of its surroundings the garden comes as a fantastic oasis of colour and warmth to the visitor. Its secret, of course, is the same as all west coast gardens – the benign influence of the Gulf Stream. In the case of Inverewe this was assisted in its work by the shelter belt of trees planted on the little headland. When this operation was started the only vegetation to be seen was a single bush of dwarf willow about three feet high. Now, Inverewe has a wealth of plant life introduced from many different countries. Something of interest can be found in the garden at any time of the year but probably spring is the most generally colourful season. There is a Trust Information Centre at the garden.
Admission. Dawn to dusk throughout the year. Adults 35p, children 5p. Coach parties 20p, car park 5p. Guidebook 15p. Licensed restaurant open April-September. Telephone Poolewe 247. Snack bar in car park.
Visitor centre. April-mid-October 10-6.30. Sunday 1-6.30.
Wardens. Lt. Commdr. J. M. C. Fenton RN (Ret'd) and Mrs Fenton, Gate Lodge, Inverewe. Tel. Poolewe 229.

Between the garden and Poolewe village the National Trust for Scotland has set up the Inverewe Stage House, in conjunction with Shell Oil Ltd., to serve as a caravan and camping site and centre of information for visitors. In addition to the laundry, drying room and showers, there is a welcome innovation – covered space for wet-weather tenting.
Wardens. Mr & Mrs R. D. Gamble (Tel. Poolewe 249). Trust representatives at Inverewe and Torridon: Mr & Mrs J. G. B. Gibson, Inverewe House, Poolewe (Tel. Poolewe 200).

RC.6. INVERPOLLY NATURE RESERVE (N.C.C.)

A wild, remote, almost uninhabited area on the north west coast of Ross and
Cromarty near the Sutherland border, which includes three summits over
2,000 feet and the whole of Loch Sionascaig. There is a great diversity of
habitats; lochs, streams, bogs, moorland, woodland, screes, cliffs and summits.
On the east boundary is the classic geological locality of Knockan Cliff, which
exposes a section of the Moine Thrust zone. Among the wild life of the area
are wildcats, pine marten, red and roe deer, and golden eagles. The Reserve
contains relatively untouched relics of primitive birch-hazel woodland.
Access as for Inchnadamph N.N.R. There is a car park and a Nature
Conservancy Council Information Centre at Knockan Cliff where a nature
trail helps to explain the geological interest of the area. A 50 mile Motor trail,
designed to add to the motorist's enjoyment and understanding of the N.W.
Highlands, starts and finishes at the car park and encompasses the entire
reserve.
*Wardens: Mr R. Tindall, Strathpolly, near Ullapool (Tel. Lochinver 204)
and Mr D. Gowans, Knockan Cottage, Elphin, by Lairg (Tel. Elphin 234).
Pamphlet "North West Scotland National Nature Reserves" 5p, available as
for Allt nan Carnan leaflet and from Wardens. Nature trail booklet 3p.
Motor trail booklet 10p.*

RC.7. Kyle of Lochalsh, BALMACARA AND KINTAIL (N.T.S.)

These two properties some ten miles apart combine the interests of crofting
agriculture and magnificent Highland scenery, including the Five Sisters
of Kintail and Beinn Fhada (Ben Attow). Places of interest have been
sign-posted, rough-hewn log tables and benches make inviting picnic places
and an Information Centre is open from June to September in Balmacara
village. The hills offer a wide choice of walks and climbs, botanical
expeditions and other naturalists' ploys. The Trust's land (over 23,000 acres)
is accessible to the public at all times but permission should be sought before
venturing on to neighbouring property. A limited number of fishing permits for
salmon, grilse and sea-trout may be obtained from Morvich Farm where there
is also a camping and caravan site. (See also Falls of Glomach).
*Trust Information Centre, Balmacara (Tel. Balmacara 236). Trust
representative: Mr W. N. Sharp, A. F. S., Lochalsh House, Kyle of Lochalsh
(Tel. Balmacara 207). Ranger-Naturalist: Mr P. MacKenna (Tel. Balmacara
278). Guided walks programme. Guidebook "Kintail, Balmacara and Falls of
Glomach", 15p from Balmacara or Trust Information Centres at Inverewe,
Torridon and Morvich. Morvich camping site, Kintail, on banks of River Croe.
Visitor Centre with audio vision. Warden: Mr R. MacLean, Morvich Farm,
Inverinate, by Kyle. Tel. Glenshiel 219.*

RC.8. Kyle of Lochalsh-Invergarry Road, FALLS OF GLOMACH (N.T.S.)

One of the highest waterfalls in Britain, Glomach has a sheer drop of 300 feet
and a further fall of 50 feet from the projecting ledge to the bottom pool. The
most used access to the falls is by the road branching off A87 at Ardelve and
signposted "To Killilan". To proceed beyond the end of the public road by car,
permission may be obtained to use the private estate road for a further
four miles by signing the visitors book at Killilan House. Motorists are warned
that this road is in parts very rough. At the point from which the footpath
to the falls starts there is a turning place for cars and a small car park. The
footpath from there is in places very steep and could be dangerous unless the
visitor is physically fit and well shod for about one hour's walking.
Alternative routes are by the Dorusduain road which branches off at the head
of Loch Duich and thence by forest roads to a small car park provided by the

Forestry Commission, from which there is a footpath for about three and a half miles to the falls – or wholly on foot from Morvich farm with alternative routes by Dorusduain and Bealach na Sgairne or by Glen Choinneachain, both of which are about six and a half miles.

Accessible at all times, except that, as stated above, the Killilan route runs through a private estate. Stalking may be in progress, particularly during August and September. Care is needed on approach paths. Guidebook, "Kintail, Balmacara and Falls of Glomach", 15p, from Balmacara (q.v.) and N.T.S. Information Centres. Guided walks programme.

RC.9. Lochcarron, ALLT NAN CARNAN NATURE RESERVE (N.C.C.)

A mile-long, thickly wooded gorge cutting through both calcareous and noncalcareous rocks. The plant life is rich and varied and the Nature Conservancy Council plans to study the relationships of the plants with rock type, shade and moisture.

Situation. 2 miles north-west of Lochcarron.
Pamphlet, "North West Scotland National Nature Reserves", 5p (N.C.C.); Warden, Anancaun, Kinlochewe (Telephone 254); Knockan N.C.C. Information Centre; N.T.S. Information Centre, Inverewe (Telephone Poolewe 206); Inverewe Stage House (Telephone 249).

RC.10. Loch Kishorn, RASSAL ASHWOOD NATURE RESERVE (N.C.C.)

This is one of the very few natural type ashwoods found in Scotland and is the most northerly in Great Britain. The floor of the wood, which is growing on limestone pavement, is remarkable in that it has a peculiar hummocky surface, rich in mosses.

Situation. East of the Lochcarron-Shieldaig road, just north of Loch Kishorn.
Pamphlet "North West Scotland National Nature Reserves" 5p. (Available as for Allt nan Carnan leaflet). Wardened from Anancaun (Beinn Eighe).

RC.11. Loch Maree, SLATTADALE FOREST TRAILS (F.C.)

A short forest trail (1½ miles) and the longer Tollie Path (5 miles) lead from a small car park and picnic area on the south-west shore of Loch Maree. The oldest part of the forest was planted in 1922 and a leaflet describes the species and wildlife. (Road improvements may cause disruption.)

Leaflet, 5p, on site and locally.
Situation. 3 miles north-west of Talladale on A832.

RC.12. Plockton, EILEAN NA CREIGE DUIBHE NATURE RESERVE
(S.W.T.)

A very attractive small island, at the mouth of Loch Carron, accessible by boat from Plockton. The island carries a stand of Scots pine in which herons nest. Visitors are asked to avoid disturbing the nesting birds and to take great care not to start fires.

RC.13. Strathpeffer, TORRACHILTY FOREST TRAIL (F.C.)

The guide to this forest trail identifies a number of tree species and also lists much of the other plant and animal life to be seen along the 3¼ mile route.

Leaflet, 5p, from Forest Office and locally.
Situation. 6 miles west of Dingwall at Contin on A834.

RC.14. TORRIDON (N.T.S.)

The 14,000 acre estate of Torridon, which includes some of the finest mountain scenery in Scotland, lies immediately to the West of the Beinn Eighe Nature Reserve (q.v.). Beinn Eighe (3,309 feet), Liathach (3,456 feet) and Beinn Alligin (3,232 feet) are among the Torridon mountains which hold much of interest to geologists and naturalists. The wild life includes red and roe deer, mountain goat, pine marten, wildcat, mountain hare, golden eagle, peregrine falcon, greylag goose, merlin, ptarmigan, grouse, ring ouzel, red and black-throated divers. The flora includes sundews, butterwort, mountain sorrel, starry and mountain saxifrage, northern rock cress. There is a Trust Information Centre and self-guided walks.

Booklet 10p from N.T.S. Information Centres, Torridon; Balmacara, Inverewe, Morvich, Kintail; and N.C. Warden, Anancaun, Kinlochewe.
Ranger Naturalist: Mr L. MacNally, The Mains Farm, Torridon (Tel. 221).
Guided Walks Programme.

ISLANDS

RC.15. Lewis, BLACK HOUSE, No 42 Arnol *(P.S.A.)*
A good example of a traditional type of Hebridean dwelling with thatched roof, central peat fire in the kitchen and no chimney.
Situation. At Arnol, 15 miles north-west of Stornoway, on the Barvas-Carloway road. O.S. 1" map sheet 8, ref. NB 311488.
Admission. Weekdays, April-September 12-2 and 5-7, October-March 12-2. Closed on Sundays. 5p.

RC.16. Lewis, CALLANISH STANDING STONES *(P.S.A.)*
A cruciform setting of megaliths unique in Scotland and outstanding in Great Britain, probably carried out in a series of additions (*c.* 2000-1500 B.C.).
Situation. On the ridge of a promontory extending into Loch Roag, about 13 miles west of Stornoway. O.S. 1" map sheet 8, ref. NB 213331.
Admission. All times without charge. Leaflet.

RC.17. Lewis, DUN CARLOWAY BROCH *(P.S.A.)*
One of the best preserved Iron Age broch towers in the Western Isles. Still standing about 30 feet high.
Situation. 1½ miles south-west of Carloway and about 15 miles west-north-west of Stornoway. O.S. 1" map sheet 8, ref. NB 190413.
Admission. All times without charge.

RC.18. Lewis, SHAWBOST MUSEUM AND MILL
In the museum in Shawbost village, items illustrating the old Lewis way of life have been collected. They include crofting, fishing and Harris Tweed weaving implements and articles, old photographs and local records. An old Norse water mill has also been restored. Both these projects were carried out under the Highland Village Competition in 1970.
Situation. The museum is on the A858, and directions to the mill are obtainable there. O.S. 1" map sheet 8, ref. NB 256465.
Admission. Free but donations welcomed.

RC.19. Lewis, "STEINACLEIT" CAIRN AND STONE CIRCLE, Barvas
(P.S.A.)
The fragmentary remains of a chambered cairn of Neolithic date (*c.* 2000 B.C.).
Situation. At the south end of Loch an Duin, Shader, 12 miles north of Stornoway, off the A857. O.S. 1" map sheet 8, ref. NB 396541.
Admission. All times without charge.

RC.20. NORTH RONA AND SULA SGEIR NATURE RESERVES *(N.C.C.)*
Uninhabited islands, situated some 44 miles north-west of Cape Wrath, which are notable for a breeding colony of grey seals and Leach's forktailed petrels. Sula Sgeir has a large colony of gannets, the traditional harvesting of which by the men of Ness is still legally authorised.
Access is restricted. Leaflet (N.C.C.).

ROXBURGHSHIRE Maps 2, 5, & 6

Ro.1. BORDER FOREST PARK *(F.C.)*

Scotland has a share in the Border Forest Park which covers 125,000 acres along the marches between Roxburghshire and Dumfriesshire and the English counties of Northumberland and Cumberland. The Scottish forests which form part of the Forest Park are Wauchope, south of Bonchester Bridge, Roxburghshire, and Newcastleton, near Newcastleton, Dumfriesshire.
Situation. Approached by unclassified road running north-east then south-east from Saughtree (NY 562968) on B6357, Longtown-Jedburgh road.
Border Guide from Forestry Commission, 55/57 Moffat Road, Dumfries DG1 1NP.

Ro.2. Hawick, TEVIOTHEAD PICNIC SITE *(Roxburgh C.C.)*

Picnic area in Teviotdale, beside the A7 trunk road about 8 miles south west of Hawick.

Ro.3. Jedburgh, ABBEY *(P.S.A.)*

A house of Augustinian canons regular, founded by David I, Jedburgh possesses the only complete, or nearly complete, Transitional west front in Scotland.
Situation. In Jedburgh. O.S. 1" map sheet 70, ref. NT 650205.
Admission. Standard. 10p. Card Guide 1p. The Scottish Border Abbeys Popular Guide is also available, price 10p.

Jedburgh, DERE STREET ROMAN ROAD

The section of Dere Street from the county boundary to Jedfoot has been signposted for walkers and information boards have been erected at strategic points. It is hoped to extend it to Melrose in the near future.
Leaflets from County Planning Department, Newtown St. Boswells; Borders Tourist Association, Kelso and Tourist Information Centre, Jedburgh.

Ro.4. Kelso, ABBEY *(P.S.A.)*

Another of David I's great foundations for the Tironensian Order. The best preserved portion is the north transept, a superb piece of design.
Situation. In Kelso. O.S. 1" map sheet 70, ref. NT 729338.
Admission. Standard without charge but notice posted when key-holder absent. Guidebook Scottish Border Abbeys, Popular Guide, 10p, and leaflet.

Ro.5. Kelso, SMAILHOLM TOWER *(P.S.A.)*

The tower, commanding a magnificent view of the Border country is 57 feet high and was probably erected in the 15th century.
Situation. Near the farm of Sandyknowe, 6 miles west of Kelso and 1½ miles south-west of Smailholm. O.S. 1" map sheet 70, ref. NT 638347.
Admission. All reasonable times without charge, on application to key-keeper, at Sandyknowe farmhouse. Leaflet.

Ro.6. Melrose, ABBEY *(P.S.A.)*

This beautiful Cistercian abbey, founded by David I, was repeatedly wrecked in the Wars of Independence. The beauty of the figure sculpture is unrivalled in Scotland.
Situation. In Melrose. O.S. 1" map sheet 70, ref. NT 549342.
Admission. Standard. 10p. Official Guide 10p. Card Guide 1p. Scottish Border Abbeys Popular Guide also available, price 10p. Tel. Melrose 262.

Melrose, THE EILDON WALK
The Eildon Walk, a circular walk round the burgh of Melrose sets out to inform
the walker of some of the history associated with the area.
*Leaflets from Melrose Town Council, Public Library, County Planning
Department, Newtown St Boswells and Borders Tourist Association, Kelso.*

Ro.7. Newcastleton, HERMITAGE CASTLE   (P.S.A.)
This vast ruin is associated with many stirring incidents. Its architectural
history is obscure: but the oldest work seems to date from the 14th century.
Situation. In Liddesdale, $5\frac{1}{2}$ miles north-east of Newcastleton.
O.S. 1" map sheet 69, ref. NY 497961.
Admission. Standard. 5p. Official Guide Book 11p.

Ro.8. Town Yetholm, YETHOLM LOCH NATURE RESERVE   (S.W.T.)
An attractive loch, noted for migratory wildfowl and breeding birds, with some
uncommon marshland plants.
*Permit required. Obtainable from the Hon. Warden , Mr J. Hamilton Brown,
Hillhouse, Kirk Yetholm, Kelso. Limited reception facilities. Parties of more
than 6 who wish to visit the reserve should book with the Warden or
Branch Secretary.*

Yetholm, THE PENNINE WAY
The Pennine Way, the national footpath from Derbyshire to the Scottish
Borders terminates at Kirk Yetholm.

SELKIRKSHIRE

Map 5

Se.1.   St Mary's Loch, KIRK

On the hillside north of the lovely St Mary's Loch is the ruined church of
St Mary's, which itself probably occupies the site of the church of St Mary
of the Lowes known to have existed in 1292.

Se.2.   St Mary's Loch, DRYHOPE TOWER

A stout little tower originally four storeys high, overlooking the Dryhope Burn.
In 1592 an order was made for its destruction and it was probably re-built
a few years later.

Se.3.   Selkirk, NEWARK CASTLE

First mentioned in 1423, the Castle of "Newark" or "New Werk" was so
called to distinguish it from the older castle of "Auldwark" which stood
nearby. The castle is an oblong tower-house, five storeys from attic to cellar,
standing within a barmkin. It was a royal hunting seat for the Forest of Ettrick
and the Royal Arms of James I are decipherable on a stone in the west gable.

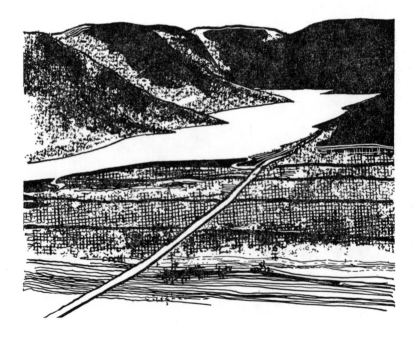

SHETLAND Map 14

MAINLAND

Sh.1. Lerwick, CLICKHIMIN BROCH (P.S.A.)
First occupied in the Bronze Age (700-500 B.C.), fortified during the Iron
Age (500-300 B.C.), and occupied into the later Iron Age.
Situation. About ¾ mile south-west of Lerwick.
O.S. 1" map sheet 4, ref. HU 464408.
Admission. Standard, without charge. Official Guide (includes Mousa) 5p.

Lerwick, FORT CHARLOTTE (P.S.A.)
The fort, roughly pentagonal in shape, was begun in 1665 to protect the
Sound of Bressay against the Dutch.
Situation. Overlooking the harbour. O.S. 1" map sheet 4, ref. HU 476418.
Admission. All times without charge.

Sh.2. Scalloway, CASTLE (P.S.A.)
A fine castellated mansion on the "two-stepped" plan, built in 1600 by the
notorious Patrick Stewart, Earl of Orkney.
Situation. In Scalloway, about 5 miles west of Lerwick.
O.S. 1" map sheet 4, ref. HU 405393.
Admission. All reasonable times without charge, on application to custodian.
Official Guide Pamphlet 2½p.

Sh.3. Sumburgh, JARLSHOF (P.S.A.)
One of the most remarkable archaeological sites in Britain, with the remains
of three extensive village settlements occupied from Bronze Age to Viking
times.
*Situation. Sumburgh Head, about 22 miles due south of Lerwick on the
southermost point of Shetland, close to Sumburgh airfield. O.S. 1" map
sheet 4, ref. HU 398096. Bus service from Lerwick to Sumburgh.*
Admission. Standard. 10p. Official Guide Book 11p.

Sumburgh, NESS OF BURGI (P.S.A.)
A defensive stone-built structure of Iron Age date which is related in certain
features to the brochs.
*Situation. On the coast at the tip of Scatness, about 1 mile south-west of
Jarlshof, at the south end of the mainland of Shetland. O.S. 1" map sheet 4,
ref. HU 388084.*
Admission. All times without charge.

Sh.4. Voe, Dunrossness, CROFT HOUSE MUSEUM
(County of Zetland Museum Management Committee)
A Shetland croft house, renovated and refurnished in the style typical of a
century ago, with its associated farm buildings and water mill.
Situation. Half a mile south of Boddam, South Mainland.
O.S. 1" map sheet 4, ref. HU 398148.
*Admission. Open daily (except Monday) 10-1 and 2-5 from 1st May to
30 September. Admission 10p, children 5p.*

SHETLAND

Sh.5. Walls, STANEYDALE

m

A Neolithic structure, heel-shaped externally, and containing a large oval chamber (*c.* 1600 B.C.).
Situation. 2¾ miles east-north-east of Walls. O.S. 1" map sheet 2, ref. HU 285503.
Admission. All times without charge. Access is through boggy ground.

OTHER ISLANDS

Sh.6. FAIR ISLE

(N.T.S.)

☆

The name of Fair Isle is well known throughout the world for original studies carried out on migrating birds. The island, which seems to be a staging post for migrants, has an extraordinary record of about 300 species observed. The main problem affecting the island is the tendency, universal in remote areas, towards de-population. In a successful effort to stem the drift away, the National Trust for Scotland has encouraged improvements in housing and some of the other basic amenities. Fair Isle has great charm, peace and varied interest to offer the visitor. It has, too, a great tradition of hospitality. Although in some ways the most isolated inhabited island in Britain, Fair Isle is reasonably accessible to the visitor by both air and sea, and there is accommodation in the new observatory hostel (open March-November).
Details from the Warden, Fair Isle Bird Observatory, Fair Isle, Shetland; the Fair Isle Bird Observatory Trust, 21 Regent Terrace, Edinburgh EH7 5BN, or from the N.T.S., 5 Charlotte Square, Edinburgh EH2 4DU.
Guidebook 15p from W. S. Wilson, Stackhoull Stores, Fair Isle or from N.T.S. Trust Representative: Mr S. Thomson, Sen., Shirva, Fair Isle (Tel. Fair Isle 1).

Sh.7. Fetlar, NATURE RESERVE

(R.S.P.B.)

Between 15th April and 15th August, access is strictly limited to path leading to Observation Post for viewing a pair of snowy owls which have nested each year since 1967. *Visitors should contact the R.S.P.B. Summer Warden at Bealance House, Fetlar. (Telephone Fetlar 246.)*

Sh.8. HAAF GRUNEY NATURE RESERVE

(N.C.C.)

This is a small uninhabited island, lying about 3 miles south-east of Uyeasound. Landing is possible only in calm weather. It is a low, green, fertile islet, with a flora resembling that of similar areas of serpentine rock on Unst. Chromite was at one time mined and storm petrels breed in the debris from the shafts.

Sh.9. Mousa, BROCH

(P.S.A.)

m

The best preserved example of the remarkable Iron Age broch towers peculiar to Scotland. The tower still stands to a height of over 40 feet all round.
Situation. On the west shore of the island of Mousa, which is off the east coast of the mainland of Shetland. O.S. 1" map sheet 4, ref. HU 457237.
Access by hire of boat from the village of Sandwick (telephone Mr Jamieson, Sandwick 367) about 14 miles south of Lerwick. Daily bus service from Lerwick and Sandwick.
Admission. All times without charge. Official Guide Book 5p (includes Clickhimin). (Available at Jarlshof and from boatman).

Sh.10. NOSS NATURE RESERVE

(N.C.C. and R.S.P.B.)

A spectacular seabird sanctuary. A sheep-grazed island rising abruptly to the east with vertical sea cliffs culminating in the magnificent bird cliff of the Noup (592 feet). All the typical Shetland sea birds.
Access. RSPB warden based on Noss will row visitors across Noss Sound from Bressay. Visitors wishing to go across to island should get details beforehand from the information office at Lerwick. Boats from Lerwick do trips round Noss — advertised locally.

Sh.11.   Unst, HERMANESS NATURE RESERVE   *(N.C.C.)*

The scientific interest of the Reserve is largely ornithological. It is an important breeding station of the great skua, a bird with a very restricted distribution in the northern hemisphere, and arctic skuas and red-throated divers breed also on the peninsula. The sea cliffs hold an expanding gannetry and also colonies of kittiwakes and puffins. Muckle Flugga, the Outstack and the north-west corner of Unst are included in the Reserve. There is no Warden and there are no restrictions on access.

Inquiries should be made to the Assistant Regional Officer, East Scotland, J. L. Johnstone, Brake, Bigton, Shetland.

Sh.12.   Unst, MUNESS CASTLE   *(P.S.A.)*

Late 16th century building, rubble built, but with exceptionally fine architectural detail.

Situation. At the south end of the island of Unst. O.S. 1″ map sheet 1, ref. HP 629013. Access from Lerwick by steamer or overland by bus and ferry.
Admission. All reasonable times without charge on application to key-keeper. Leaflet.

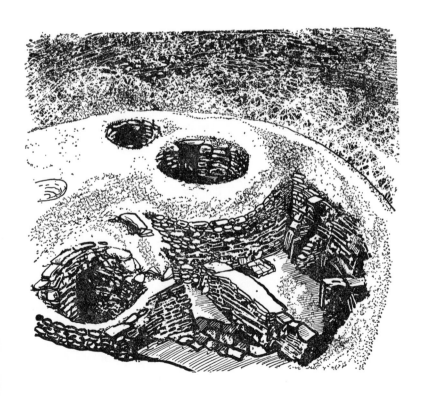

St.1. Airth, HAUGH OF AIRTH PICNIC SITE *(Stirling C.C.)*
Picnic area beside the A876 road about 1 mile south of the Kincardine Bridge.

St.2. ANTONINE WALL AND ASSOCIATED WORKS *(P.S.A.)*
Three outstanding lengths of the Antonine Wall, and one wall-fort, are in the custody of the Department. These are (from east to west):
1. Watling Lodge. Visible remains of the rampart have been destroyed by agriculture, but the profile of the ditch retains its original V-section.
Situation. 1½ miles west of centre of Falkirk, on B816. O.S. 1" map sheet 61, ref. NS 862798.

2. Rough Castle, Roman fort and adjacent length of rampart and ditch. One of the most notable Roman military sites in Britain. A unique feature is the series of defensive pits, lilia, outside the Antonine ditch.
Situation. 1½ miles east of Bonnybridge. O.S. 1" map sheet 61, ref. NS 843799.

3. Seabegs Wood. A good length of rampart and ditch.
Situation. 1¼ miles south-west of Bonnybridge, beside B816. O.S. 1" map sheet 61, ref. NS 814793.
Admission. All times without charge.

St.3. Auchineden, "QUEEN'S VIEW" & PICNIC SITE *(Stirling C.C.)*
Here Queen Victoria in 1869 had her first view of Loch Lomond, "Queen of the Scottish Lochs". The view extends from Argyll peaks to Fintry Hills. The National Trust for Scotland has marked a route for visitors to reach the curious chasm known as "THE WHANGIE". 1½ miles by path.
Situation. About 5 miles west of Blanefield, off Milngavie-Drymen road.

St.4. Balmaha, PICNIC SITE *(F.C.)*
Picnic area by B837 road at Balmaha with access to viewpoint and forest trail.

Balmaha, MANSE BAY PICNIC SITE
Picnic area about ½ mile north-west of Balmaha.

Balmaha, MILARROCHY PICNIC SITE *(Stirling C.C.)*
Picnic area about 1½ miles north-west of Balmaha.

Balmaha, SALLOCHIE PICNIC SITE *(F.C.)*
Picnic area in Rowardennan Forest, about 3½ miles north-west of Balmaha. Access to forest trail.

St.5. BANNOCKBURN MONUMENT *(N.T.S.)*
The Borestone at Bannockburn is by tradition the spot where Robert Bruce, King of Scots raised his standard before the battle of 1314. There will probably always remain a conflict of opinion about the precise site and the attendant detail of the encounter. In brief, the forces of Robert Bruce intercepted, outmanoeuvred and decisively defeated the army of Edward II on its way to relieve Stirling Castle where an English Governor was besieged. The victory regained for Scotland her freedom and national independence and has a unique significance in the nation's history. The site is now marked by a rotunda erected by the National Trust for Scotland and an equestrian statue of the Bruce by Mr C. d'O. Pilkington Jackson, erected by the King Robert the

Bruce Memorial Fund. There is a Trust Information Centre and audio-visual presentation of the Wars of Independence, culminating in the battle itself, entitled "The Forging of a Nation".
Admission. Display open weekdays April, May, June, September–mid-October, 10–6: July-August, 10–7: Sundays 11–7. Adults 25p, children 5p. Parking 10p. Guide book 10p. Tel. Bannockburn 2664.

St.6. Buchlyvie, PICNIC SITE   *(Stirling C.C.)*
Picnic area beside A811 road at east end of Buchlyvie.

Buchlyvie, BALWILL PICNIC SITE   *(Stirling C.C.)*
Picnic site by A811 road about 2 miles west of Buchlyvie.

St.7. Gargunnock, REDHALL PICNIC SITE   *(Stirling C.C.)*
Picnic area by A811 road about 2 miles east of Gargunnock.

St.8. Inversnaid, PICNIC SITE   *(Stirling C.C.)*
Picnic area at "the end of the road" (B829) from Aberfoyle to Loch Lomond; near passenger ferry pier.

Inversnaid, GARRISON OF INVERSNAID PICNIC SITE/VIEWPOINT
(Stirling C.C.)
Picnic site about half-way between the west end of Loch Arklet and Inversnaid by the shore of Loch Lomond.

LOCH LOMOND NATURE RESERVE (see Dunbartonshire).

QUEEN ELIZABETH FOREST PARK (see Perthshire).

St.9. Rowardennan, PICNIC SITE   *(F.C.)*
Picnic area on east bank of Loch Lomond; near start of Ben Lomond walk and passenger ferry pier.

Rowardennan, LOCHAN MAOILL DHUINNE PICNIC SITE   *(F.C.)*
Picnic area by shore of Loch Lomond about ¾ mile south-east of Rowardennan.

St.10. Stirling, CAMBUSKENNETH ABBEY   *(P.S.A.)*
Founded in 1147 by David I as a house of Augustinian Canons and the scene of Bruce's important Parliament in 1326.
Situation. 1 mile east of Stirling. O.S. 1" map sheet 54, ref. NS 809939.
Admission. Standard, but closed in winter. 5p. Official Guide Pamphlet 1p.
(Available at Stirling Castle).

Stirling, "THE KING'S KNOT"   *(P.S.A.)*
One of the earliest ornamental gardens in Scotland, this "knot" garden was devised with a layout of lawns and terraces with earthen mounds and ramps.
Situation. Below and to the west of the castle rock, by A811. Clearly visible from the castle ramparts. O.S. 1" map sheet 54, ref. NS 789936.
Admission. All times without charge.

Stirling, LANDMARK   (Visitor Centres Ltd.)
An exhibition of 19th century photographs and an audio-visual programme effectively bring alive the Stirling of the past. From the outlook windows there are panoramic views of the Carse of Stirling and the hills beyond.
Situation. At the foot of the Castle Esplanade.
Admission. Mid-March-mid-October, open daily 9 am-10 pm; mid-October-mid-March, Mon. to Fri., 10-4, Sat. and Sun. 10-5. Adults 25p, children 12½p.

SUTHERLAND

Maps 9 & 12

Su.1.   Bettyhill, INVERNAVER NATURE RESERVE   *(N.C.C.)*

Near the mouth of the River Naver. The importance of this Reserve lies in
the fact that within a small compass it contains not only a wide variety of
habitats, including those on the blown sand, but also the finest assemblage
of northern plant communities in the North of Scotland.
Hon. Warden: W. Mackay, 89 Invernaver, Bettyhill, Sutherland.

Su.2.   Bonar Bridge, KYLE OF SUTHERLAND FOREST WALKS   *(F.C.)*

Four walks, with good viewpoints, traverse forest roads and paths on either side
of the Kyle of Sutherland. A booklet, with maps, describes the routes (5p).
There is no car park at the Invershin section.
Situation: (1) Carbisdale Castle on Ardgay-Inveroykel road.
         (2) 1 mile north of Bonar on A836.
         (3) 3 miles north of Bonar on A836.
         (4) Opposite Shin Falls on Lairg-Inveran road 4½ miles south of Lairg.

Su.3.   Durness, SMOO CAVES

The caves, at the end of a deep cleft in the limestone cliffs, consist of three
chambers. The entrance to the first resembles a Gothic arch. The second
cavern, difficult of access, has a waterfall.
Situation. 2 miles east of Durness.

Su.4.   Golspie, LOCH FLEET NATURE RESERVE   *(S.W.T.)*

A large sea loch with extensive tidal flats and varied shore habitats together
with adjoining dune grasslands and pine woodlands. Considerable
ornithological interest in summer and winter seasons; the typical pine
woodland flora is rich and varied. Most of the reserve is open to Trust
members and their guests but *permits are required for entry to Ferry Links
Wood and prior arrangements are necessary for organised parties. Application
should be made to the Sutherland Estates Office, Golspie.*

Su.5.   INCHNADAMPH NATURE RESERVE   *(N.C.C.)*

The Reserve lies in a tract of great geological and physiographical interest.
At Beinn nan Cnaimhseag an isolated outcrop of Torridon sandstone rests
upon the Durness limestone. The limestone runs in ridges, separated by
peat-covered hollows, partly clothed in willow scrub of a type common in
Scandinavia but hitherto undescribed in Scotland. It includes the Karst type
of limestone country with sink-holes, underground streams and limestone
caves. The famous Allt nan Uamh bone caves contain Paleolithic cave
earths with a fauna of Pleistocene mammals and traces of occupation by
early man. Authority required to visit in late summer and autumn and for
parties of more than six at any time.
Hon. Warden, J. Mackenzie, Stronchrubie, Inchnadamph. (Tel. Assynt 208).
Pamphlet, "North West Scotland National Nature Reserves", 3p. (N.C.C.)

SUTHERLAND

Su.6. Tongue, BORGIE FOREST WALK (F.C.)

The forest which is one of the oldest Commission woods in Scotland lies in the valley of the Borgie River and is a sheltered oasis on the exposed north coast. The walk moves through the oldest plantations with pleasant open glades for picnicking.
Situation. At forest entrance on A836 Tongue-Bettyhill road about 6 miles east of Tongue.

ISLANDS

Su.7. HANDA NATURE RESERVE (R.S.P.B.)

An island seabird sanctuary lying three miles north-west of Scourie. Vast numbers of fulmars, shags, gulls, kittiwakes and auks. Arctic and great skuas on moorland.
Access. Day visits by local boatmen. Accommodation in well-equipped bothy available to members of the R.S.P.B.

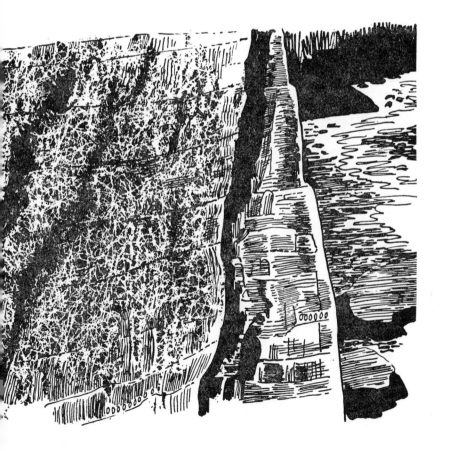

WEST LOTHIAN

Maps 4 & 5

WL.1.   Bathgate, CAIRNPAPPLE HILL: SANCTUARY BURIAL CAIRNS
(P.S.A.)

A remarkable series of ceremonial and burial monuments spanning at least
500 years (*c.* 2000–1500 B.C.); recently excavated and laid out.
*Situation. About 1½ miles east of Torphichen and 3 miles north of Bathgate.
O.S. 1" map sheet 61, ref. NS 987718.
Admission. April-September, standard. On weekdays in winter by
arrangement with custodian at Torphichen Preceptory; Saturdays and
Sundays, standard. 5p. Official Guide Pamphlet 2½p.*

WL.2.   Bathgate, TORPHICHEN PRECEPTORY
(P.S.A.)

This was the principal Scottish seat of the Knights Hospitallers and it shows
the martial style of ecclesiastical architecture prevalent in Scotland in the
15th century.
*Situation. In the village of Torphichen, 2½ miles north of Bathgate.
O.S. 1" map sheet 61, ref. NS 969725.
Admission. Standard. 5p. Note: Custodian is also custodian of Cairnpapple
Hill. Leaflet 1p.*

WL.3.   Bo'ness, KINNEIL HOUSE
(P.S.A.)

The part under guardianship contains important 16th and 17th century mural
and ceiling decorations.
*Situation. 1½ miles west of Bo'ness, at south side of Grangemouth road.
O.S. 1" map sheet 61, ref. NS 983806.
Admission. April-September, weekdays 9.30-7, Sundays, 2-7.
October-March, weekdays 12-4, Sundays, 2-4. 5p. Leaflet 1p.*

Bo'ness, HOPETOUN HOUSE NATURE TRAIL   *(Hopetoun Estate/S.W.T.)*

"Habitat" describes a trail through the grounds of Hopetoun House. It
identifies natural and semi-natural habitats along the route and describes the
plant and animal communities found in them.
*Booklet 15p (postage extra) on site or from S.W.T. Open May-September
inclusive.*

WL.4.   Linlithgow, BLACKNESS CASTLE
(P.S.A.)

Once one of the most important fortresses in Scotland dating from the
15th century, used in the 17th century as a prison for Covenanters.
*Situation. 4 miles north-east of Linlithgow. O.S. 1" map sheet 61,
ref. NT 055803.
Admission. Standard. 10p. Leaflet 1p.*

Linlithgow, THE HOUSE OF THE BINNS
(N.T.S.)

The House of The Binns is one of the most "lived-in" of the historic homes
open to visitors in Scotland. It has been occupied continuously by the
Dalyell family for more than three and a half centuries, and is still very much
a family home. It reflects the early 17th century transition in Scottish
architecture from the fortified stronghold to the more spacious and gracious
mansion. Magnificent moulded plaster ceilings, in deep relief, in four of the

main rooms were added between 1612 and 1630. The Binns was the home of
General Tom Dalyell who defeated the Covenanters at Rullion Green and
raised the Royal Scots Greys there in 1681.
*Admission. Easter-September, daily 2-5.30, except Friday. Adults 20p,
children 5p. Guide book 10p. Special parties by arrangement. (Members of
the Royal Scots Dragoon Guards, successors to "The Greys", in uniform are
admitted free.) Viewpoint. Visitor's trail with leaflet.
Ranger-naturalist service on Sat. afternoons. Tel. Philipstoun 255.*

Linlithgow, LITTLE HOUSES, 44 and 48 High Street (N.T.S.)

Two of the oldest houses in the old burgh of Linlithgow, making one of
the few domestic links with the 16th and early 17th centuries when the
Scottish court visited the Palace. Although small, their distinctive architecture
makes them readily identifiable on the north side of the main street. Three
storeys and a garret high, they are typical of their period with narrow
crow-stepped gables facing the street. Not open to visitors.

Linlithgow, PALACE (P.S.A.)

The oldest part of the existing ruin dates from soon after 1400. The
architecture of all periods is marked by exceptional richness and beauty.
*Situation. At Linlithgow, on the south shore of the Loch.
O.S. 1" map sheet 61, ref. NT 003774.
Admission. Standard. 10p. Official Guide Book 11p. Tel. Linlithgow 2065.*

WIGTOWNSHIRE

Maps 1 & 4

Wi.1. Glenluce, ABBEY *(P.S.A.)*

A Cistercian house, founded in 1192, of much architectural distinction and interest.
Situation. 2 miles north-west of Glenluce village. O.S. 1" map sheet 79, ref. NX 185587.
Admission. Standard. 5p. Leaflet.

Glenluce, CASTLE OF PARK *(P.S.A.)*

This tall and imposing castellated mansion, still entire, was built, according to an inscription on its walls, by Thomas Hay of Park in 1590.
Situation. ¾ mile west of Glenluce village. O.S. 1" map sheet 79, ref. NX 189571.
Admission. Not yet open to the public. May be viewed from the outside.

Wi.2. Kirkmadrine, CHURCH: EARLY CHRISTIAN STONES *(P.S.A.)*

Three of the earliest Christian monuments in Britain, showing the Chi-Rho symbol and inscriptions dating from the 5th or early 6th century.
Situation. In the Rhinns of Galloway, 1½ miles south-west of Sandhead and 7½ miles south of Stranraer. O.S. 1" map sheet 79, ref. NX 081484.
Admission. All times without charge. Official Guide Book. See under Whithorn Priory (Wi.7).

Wi.3. Monreith, FRONT BAY PICNIC SITE *(Wigtown C.C.)*

Picnic area near sandy beach with safe bathing and adjacent to golf course. Access from A747 road about 1 mile south-east of Monreith.

Wi.4. Port William, BARSALLOCH FORT *(P.S.A.)*

The fort is formed by a deep ditch with a mound on each side; in horseshoe form. The ditch measures 33 feet in width by 12 feet in depth.
Situation. On the hill above the road at Barsalloch Point, ¾ mile west of Monreith. O.S. 1" map sheet 80, ref. NX 347412.
Admission. All times without charge.

Port William, BIG BALCRAIG AND CLACHAN *(P.S.A.)*

Two groups of cup-and-ring engravings of Bronze Age date carved on the natural rock.
Situation. 2¼ miles east of Port William, north of B7021. O.S. 1" map sheet 80, ref. NX 374440 and 376445.
Admission. All times without charge.

Port William, CHAPEL FINIAN *(P.S.A.)*

A small chapel or oratory, probably of 10th-11th century date, suggesting comparisons with the small early chapels found notably in Ireland.
Situation. 5 miles north-west of Port William, on the main Glenluce road. O.S. 1" map sheet 79, ref. NX 278489.
Admission. All times without charge.

Port William, DRUCHTAG MOTEHILL   (P.S.A.)
The earthwork mound of an early medieval castle, with some traces of stone
buildings.
*Situation. In Mochrum village, 2 miles north-north-east of Port William.
O.S. 1" map sheet 80, ref. NX 349466.
Admission. All times without charge.*

Port William, DRUMTRODDAN   (P.S.A.)
A group of cup-and-ring markings of Bronze Age date on a natural rock face,
and 400 yards to the south an alignment of three adjacent surviving stones.
*Situation. On Drumtroddan Farm, 1¾ miles north-east of Port William on
the Wigtown road (A714). O.S. 1" map sheet 80, ref. NX 363447.
Admission. All times without charge.*

Port William, MONREITH CROSS   (P.S.A.)
A notable free-standing wheel-headed cross with interlaced enrichment,
7 feet 6 inches high.
*Situation. In the grounds of Monreith House about 1¾ miles south-east of
Port William. O.S. 1" map sheet 80, ref. NX 355429.
Admission. All reasonable times without charge.*

Port William, THE "WREN'S EGG" STONE CIRCLE   (P.S.A.)
The remains of a standing stone circle, originally a double concentric ring.
Only three stones remain, including the central one.
*Situation. 2 miles south-east of Port William near the farmhouse of
Blairbuie. O.S. 1" map sheet 80, ref. NX 361420.
Admission. All times without charge.*

Wi.5.   Sandhead, ARDWELL PICNIC SITE   (Wigtown C.C.)
Picnic area, overlooking Luce Bay beside the A716 road about 3½ miles south of
Sandhead.

Wi.6.   Stranraer, BALYETT PICNIC SITE   (Wigtown C.C.)
Picnic area by the shore of Loch Ryan, about 1 mile north-east of Stranraer
on the A77 road.

Wl.7.   Whithorn, PRIORY   (P.S.A.)
The first Christian church in Scotland was founded here by St Ninian in the
5th century. The medieval church was founded in the 12th century.
*Situation. At Whithorn. O.S. 1" map sheet 80, ref. NX 445403.
Admission. Standard. 5p. Official Guide Book 11p. The Guide Book to
Early Christian and Pictish Monuments of Scotland is also available, price 25p.*

Whithorn, RISPAIN CAMP   (P.S.A.)
A rectangular enclosure defined by double banks and ditches. Probably
a medieval homestead site.
*Situation. 1 mile west of Whithorn near Rispain Farm.
O.S. 1" map sheet 80, ref. NX 429399.
Admission. All times without charge.*

Wi.8.   Whithorn, ST NINIAN'S CAVE   *(P.S.A.)*

m   This cave might well have been St Ninian's place of retreat, as within there
has been found a fine assemblage of early Christian crosses.
*Situation. Physgill, on the coast 4 miles south-west of Whithorn. Footpath
¾ mile from Kidsdale Farm. O.S. 1" map sheet 80, ref. NX 422360.
Admission. All times without charge. Official Guide Book: described in
Whithorn Priory Guide Book, 11p.*

Wi.9.   Whithorn, ST NINIAN'S CHAPEL   *(P.S.A.)*

✝   The ruins of a chapel of 13th century date. Excavations have failed to
produce evidence of an earlier church.
*Situation. The Isle of Whithorn, about 5 miles south-east of Whithorn.
O.S. 1" map sheet 80, ref. NX 479362.
Admission. All times without charge. Official Guide Book: described in
Whithorn Priory Guide Book, 11p.*

Wi.10.   Wigtown, KILSTURE FOREST WALK   *(F.C.)*

This one mile walk, which starts from a car park, has been laid out to inform
the visitor of the variety of tree species that the forester might plant and of
his reasons for choosing them.
*Situation. Bareagle Forest off Kirkinner-Sorbie road A747, 4 miles south of
Wigtown.
Booklet 10p from: F.C., Creebridge District Office, Newton Stewart and from
Warden's shop, Caldon's Camp, Glentrool.*

Wi.11.   Wigtown, STANDING STONES OF TORHOUSE   *(P.S.A.)*

m   A circle of 19 boulders standing on the edge of a low mound. Probably
Bronze Age.
*Situation. About 3½ miles west of Wigtown and on the south side of B733.
O.S. 1" map sheet 80, ref. NX 383565. Admission. All times without charge.*

Atlas Section

■ **Places of interest described in the guide**

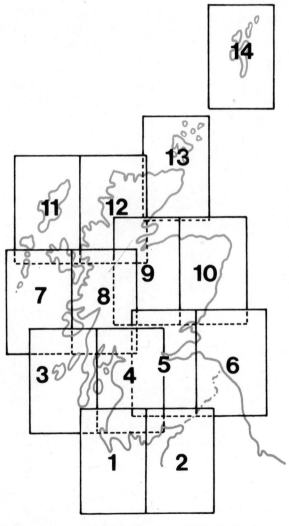

Atlas Maps: scale 12 miles = one inch approx.

10   0   10

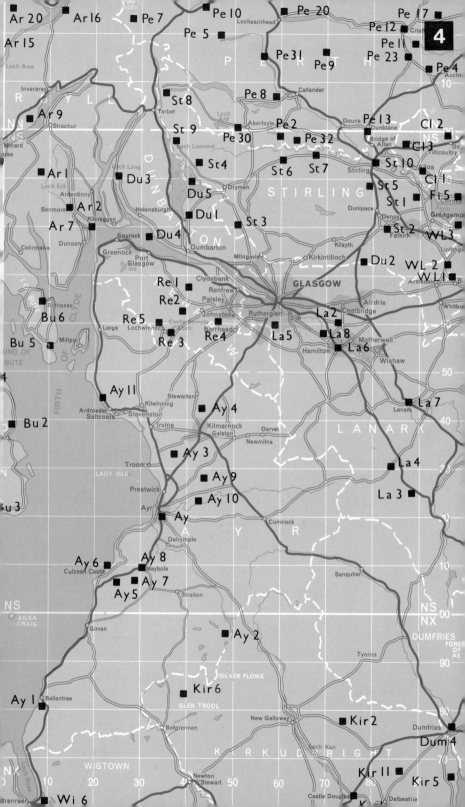

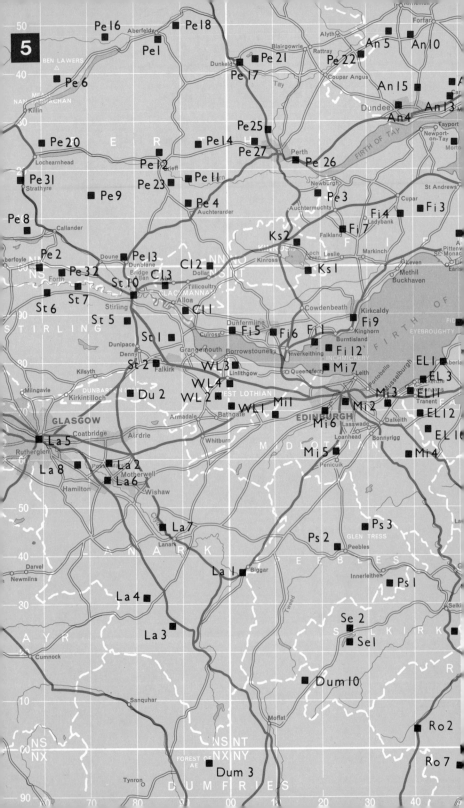

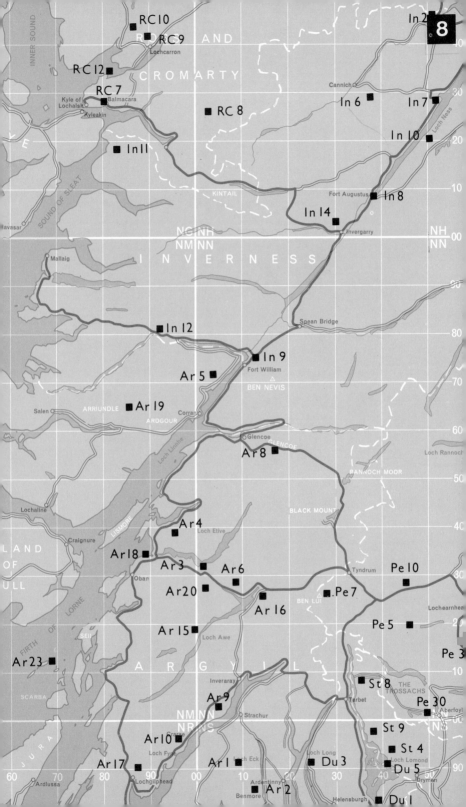

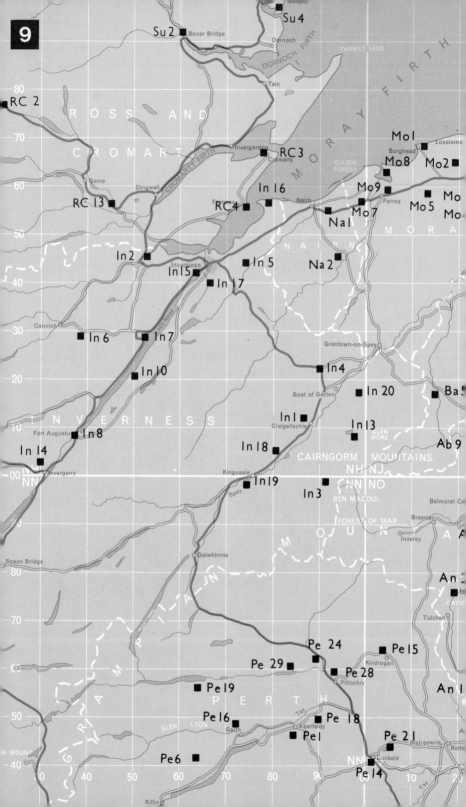

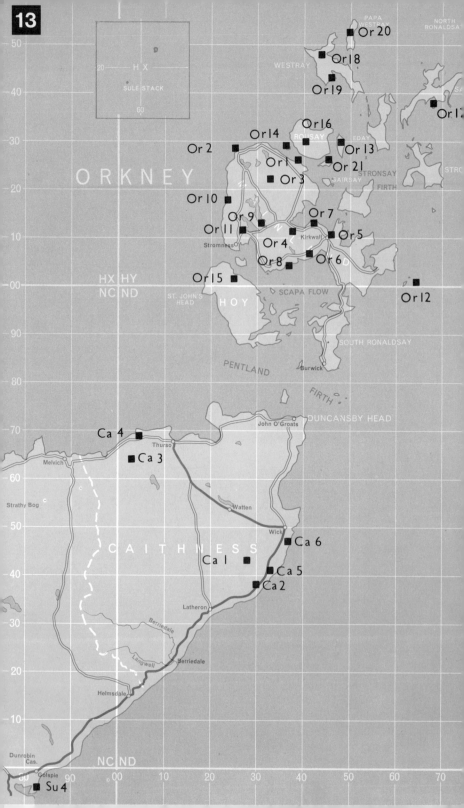

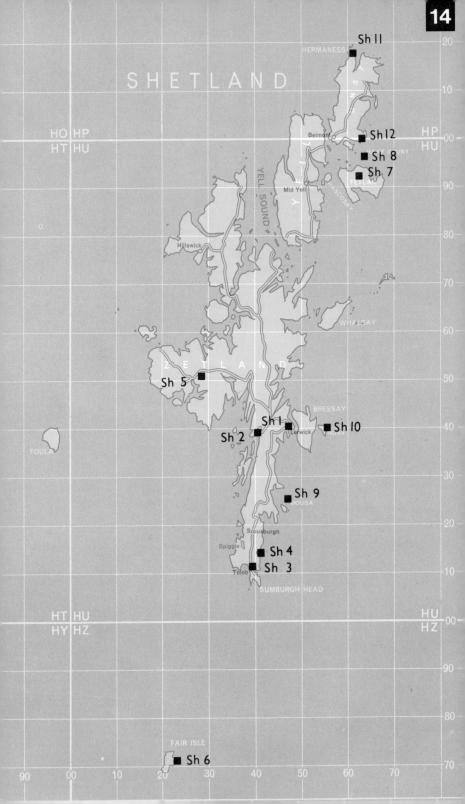